WHEN WORDS COLLIDE

A JOURNALIST'S GUIDE TO GRAMMAR AND STYLE

SECOND EDITION

LAUREN KESSLER

DUNCAN MCDONALD

School of Journalism
University of Oregon

Wadsworth Publishing Company
Belmont, California
A Division of Wadsworth, Inc.

COMMUNICATION EDITOR   Kristine Clerkin
EDITORIAL ASSISTANT   Melissa Harris
PRODUCTION EDITOR   Vicki Friedberg
DESIGNER   Julia Scannell
PRINT BUYER   Karen Hunt
COPY EDITOR   Zipporah W. Collins
COMPOSITOR   Weimer Typesetting Company
COVER   Julia Scannell
SIGNING REPRESENTATIVE   John Block

Printed in the United States of America   34

1 2 3 4 5 6 7 8 9 10—92 91 90 89 88

Library of Congress Cataloging-in-Publication Data

Kessler, Lauren.
   When words collide.

   Includes index.
   1. English language—Grammar—1950–   .
2. Journalism—Style manuals.   I. McDonald, Duncan.
II. Title.
PE1112.K435   1988   428.2′024097   87-20962
ISBN 0-534-08574-1

PREFACE

Language binds us together.

The symbols and sounds we so casually arrange as we speak or write direct our lives and connect us to each other. Through communication, our most human of acts, we learn and grow. We establish relationships, conduct business, exchange information and express emotions. When we are successful communicators, it is because we select and use language based on shared understandings and common conventions. Grammar, the common conventions that govern the way we use language, helps us communicate effectively with each other.

Some of us want to do more. We want to communicate with *millions* of people at once. We are (or aspire to be) professional communicators—reporters, editors, broadcasters, advertising specialists, public relations practitioners—and we use language daily to inform, analyze, educate, persuade and entertain. Our success depends on many things, not the least of which is our ability to articulate information by arranging language in coherent patterns. Grammar, this arrangement, is at the heart of effective mass communications.

As mass communicators, we are guardians of our language. What we write and broadcast, and how we craft our messages, can have profound effects on our readers and viewers. If we use a word incorrectly, misspell it or commit a grammatical error, our mistake is magnified by the vast reach of the medium. Our mistakes can—and have—become gospel for our audience. Because we have the power to corrupt language, we have the responsibility to uphold its worthy conventions.

When Words Collide is a grammar book for practicing and would-be mass communicators. This is the second edition; we believe it's even stronger and more useful than the first. In Part One, we have added a new chapter on spelling, the bugaboo of both experienced and novice writers. It offers a sensible *approach* to the vital skill of spelling well rather than focusing on lists of forgettable rules. Part One also contains chapters on parts of speech, the sentence, case, agreement, passive voice, punctuation, and clarity and conciseness. Part Two, a quick reference for grammar and word-use problems, offers many new entries. You will also find a self-test (with answers) in the appendix.

When we originally wrote *When Words Collide,* we were responding to a nationwide need we saw in students of journalistic writing. They wanted to learn to write well, but in most cases their first and last exposure to grammar was in junior high school. In college, their English classes shunned the subject. But we were also thinking of ourselves, as writers, and of our colleagues in newsrooms, magazine offices, broadcast stations and advertising and public relations firms. Professionals need to refresh and review their understanding of grammar as well.

During the past four years, we've heard from students, teachers and professionals about *When Words Collide.* Their suggestions have pointed out areas of special concern and have helped strengthen the book. Their letters show that learning and using grammar correctly is a life-long process.

We have strong feelings about the role of mass communications in society: It must be honest and thorough. We are equally fervent about how we use language to communicate these messages: It must be direct and correct. Our words must collide only in the positive sense—they must cause sparks and create energy.

ACKNOWLEDGEMENTS

We thank the following reviewers of the first and second editions for their careful reading of our manuscripts: Roberta Applegate, Kansas State University; J. W. Click, Louisiana State University; Donna Lee Dickerson, University of South Florida; Mervin Fairbanks, Brigham Young University; George A. Flynn, California State University, Fresno; Gary H. Mayer, East Texas State University; and George M. Pica, University of Missouri. We also thank the more than 30 adopters of the first edition who gave us their comments. Our special thanks go to senior Wadsworth editor Becky Hayden, who was the first to support and believe in this project, and communication editor Kris Clerkin, who urged us to write this second edition.

We thank the many teachers of journalism around the country who have class-tested *When Words Collide* and written to us of their experiences. And we thank—and would like to recognize—the thousands of students who have struggled with the complexities of the English language on the road to becoming professional mass communicators. *When Words Collide* is dedicated to them and to our families—Tom, Jane, Vanessa and Jackson—without whom this book never would have been.

LAUREN KESSLER
DUNCAN McDONALD
Eugene, Oregon

CONTENTS

CHAPTER 3

THE SENTENCE / 33

CHAPTER 4

AGREEMENT—RULES, EXCEPTIONS AND COMMON SENSE / 55

CHAPTER 5

CASE / 75

CHAPTER 6

PASSIVE VOICE / 89

CHAPTER 7

PUNCTUATION / 99

CHAPTER 8

SPELLING / 127

CHAPTER 9

CLARITY, CONCISENESS, COHERENCE / 139

Part Two

A TOPICAL GUIDE TO
WORD USE AND GRAMMAR / 163

APPENDIX:
GRAMMAR, WORD-USE
AND SPELLING EXAM / 211

INDEX / 224

PART ONE

UNDERSTANDING GRAMMAR AND STYLE

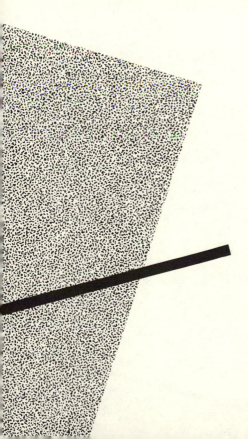

CHAPTER 1

WORDS AS TOOLS

"Grammar? What does *that* have to do with good writing?"
ask those who show—simply by asking the question—that
they know little about either.

"Everything," say good writers.

"All I know about grammar is its infinite power," writes
journalist, essayist and novelist Joan Didion. "To shift the
structure of a sentence alters the meaning of that sentence,
as definitely and inflexibly as the position of a camera alters
the meaning of the object photographed. Many people
know about cameras today, but not so many know about
sentences."

As journalists—those in large part responsible for spreading information, ideas and language throughout society—

we must know about sentences. We must know about phrases, clauses, verbs, gerunds, relative pronouns—and yes, even subordinating conjunctions.

For words are the only tools writers have. The challenge is to choose the right ones and manipulate them into patterns both coherent and graceful. To do this, we need guidelines that help us select, link and order words. We need grammar. Grammar is the system we use to combine words into larger units—phrases, clauses, sentences, paragraphs—to convey ideas and information. Grammar tells us how words relate to one another. Grammar presents the grand design that allows us to fit words together into meaningful patterns.

THE GLAMOUR OF GRAMMAR

Grammar is the systematic study of language, but this is only the most recent meaning of the word. In classical Greek and Latin, *grammar* denoted the methodical study of the entire field of literature. In the middle ages, *grammatica* was more narrowly defined as the knowledge or study of Latin, but the word slowly became synonymous with learning in general. To know *grammatica* was to be privy to all the knowledge of the learned class. This body of knowledge was, at the time, thought to include both magic and astrology. *Grammar* (or various corruptions of the word) was sometimes used as a name for these occult sciences. In fact, the word *glamour*—which first meant magic, enchantment and spell and has come to mean alluring charm—is a form of the word *grammar.*

Grammar is, in a real sense, still the study of magic. As any reader who has been transported by the written word knows, a sentence can have an overpowering and enchanting quality. But as any writer who has struggled with those words realizes, there is little sleight of hand involved. The product may be magical, but the process is just plain hard work.

Learning grammar is the first step to writing well. How can we determine which words to use and how to link them into meaningful, forceful sentences if we do not know the system? As a system of interrelated principles and procedures, grammar imposes order, logic and precision on the language. Grammar, like the process of writing itself, is a discipline demanding attention to detail and settling for nothing less than perfection. Grammar is, therefore, not only the basis for good writing but also a microcosm of the entire writing process.

THE WRITER AS WORDSMITH

Consider writing as a craft, with words as tools of the trade. Master carpenters choose the right tool for each job. They do not try to build a fine oak cabinet using an old saw and a handful of rusty nails. They collect the finest tools they can afford and learn the capabilities of each instrument. Master carpenters care for and respect their tools. So too must writers. Words are our tools, and there is, indeed, the right word for each job. Learning grammar is learning how to choose these words and connect them with precision.

Fine artisans have their self-respect tied up in the quality of their craft. A good potter, for example, is meticulous about the composition of the clay, the temperature of the kiln, the color and consistency of the glazes. This care, this craftsmanship, far exceeds what is required to produce an adequate, usable pot. To approach writing as a craft, then, is to go beyond correctness.

Tom Paine, the Revolutionary War journalist, *could* have written:

Men's souls are tried by these times.

or

These times are trying to men's souls.

But he was a craftsman, a wordsmith. He wanted to do more than produce an adequate, usable sentence. He wanted drama, cadence and rhythm. Like the master carpenter and the meticulous potter, he knew the tools of his craft and took great pride in using them well. He wrote:

These are the times that try men's souls

and more than 200 years have not diminished the power of that sentence.

Diverse crafts—writing, pottery, carpentry—have the same requirements: self-discipline, a knowledge of the medium and its tools, an ability to solve problems and pride in one's work. The first step to craftsmanship in writing is a mastery of grammar. But learning rules in a vacuum is not the way to do it. Writers serious about their craft learn the structure of language by using it—writing—and by studying how others use it—reading.

More Reasons
to Learn Grammar

Consider the plight of journalists. In the swirl of information gathering, harried journalists are expected to extract, analyze and select items that will inform, stimulate and entertain an equally harried and often distracted audience. Simultaneously, communications specialists face another challenge: correct, concise use of the language.

Every day, with every story they write, journalists face a series of grammar tests. Each word, each phrase, each sentence present journalists with choices: *Who* or *whom? That* or *which? Singular* or *plural?* Some of the choices are straightforward questions of grammar, word use and style. Others are tests of the writer's ability to use words purposefully and powerfully. To spend too long on these daily tests—looking up grammatical rules the writer has never bothered to learn—is to steal time away from the essential information-gathering process. For journalists, time is *always* in short supply.

To fail these grammar tests is to fail to communicate what may be vital information to the audience. Grammatical mistakes and word-use errors create barriers to clear communication.

Read this effort by a novice journalism student:

Expensive dormitory contracts, and there are higher student fees and buying health insurance is almost too costly for many of today's students, plus books and supplies. Searching for loans and financial aid. That's what many students have to do these days.

What is the writer trying to say here? College costs are skyrocketing, and students are looking for help in meeting them. It is an interesting story idea, but poor language use garbles the message and makes readers struggle to understand the meaning.

Here is a paragraph written by a professional news reporter:

The next legislative session could amend this situation. But if it does not, and, in the meantime, how does one select a reliable guide from what is becoming a service glutted with afterwork moonlighters and fishermen trying to turn avocation into vocation.

Poor structure and unclear writing are not monopolized by students.

With all the other demands on readers' time, would they work this hard to understand a writer's meaning?

The answer is clear: Shabby grammar, random punctuation and haphazard mechanics can cost writers their audience. When we do not follow rules that give order to our language, we confuse, bore and lose our audience. And why write if we can't be read?

Grammatical and mechanical mistakes can have other consequences for the writer. Suppose we lose not our readers but their respect? Imagine a reader picking up the daily newspaper and reading that the mayor has absconded with a million dollars from the city treasury. But the journalist who wrote the story misspelled the mayor's name. In the second sentence the subject and verb don't agree. In the third sentence there's a dangling modifier.

The reader thinks: If journalists are this careless with words, could they also be careless with facts? If journalists lack integrity as wordsmiths, could they also lack integrity as information-gatherers? Credibility means everything to journalists, and we risk losing it by misusing the language.

In fact, we risk losing our jobs or not getting them in the first place.

Listen to what prospective employers have to say about the skill of writing well:

"If I see a misspelled word on a resume, or a grammatical error, I look no further. I immediately disqualify the applicant," says the personnel director of a large company.

"We look at how much attention a person pays to detail," says the vice president of a major advertising firm. "Things like grammar, spelling and mechanics mean a lot to us. We figure, if the person can't accomplish these things, how can we expect him or her to move on to the bigger jobs?"

"What I look for in the stories that are submitted to me," says a newspaper editor, "is the ability of the writer to communicate clearly and simply. If I find grammatical and mechanical errors in the first paragraph, I stop reading. If a person can't use grammar correctly, it says either of two things to me: lack of intelligence or extreme sloppiness. Either way, it's not a person I want writing for me."

MAKING MISTAKES

What is both exciting and challenging about learning how to write is that the learning never stops. Writing well is a lifelong process. That means throughout our lives as journalists we will make mistakes: stories missed, judgments miscalled, questions unasked and language misused. Errors can be disheartening. But if we are serious about our craft, these errors can also spur us on to further learning.

As the three prospective employers have just told us, grammatical errors can be particularly dangerous. This is why *editing* and *rewriting* are vital to the process of writing. Even experienced journalists make language errors, but they *edit* their work carefully. The errors rarely make their way into print.

Begin with a solid understanding of the language. Then *edit, edit, edit*. The misspelled word on the resume and the grammatical error in the first paragraph of the story are mistakes anyone can make the first time around. Careful editing means you have the chance to improve your writing the second or third time around.

WHEN WORDS COLLIDE

When words collide, they can collide like trucks on a highway, causing chaos and damage. Or they can collide like atoms of uranium, releasing power and force. Grammatical errors cause words to collide with disastrous results. Grammatical mastery—craftsmanship—causes words to collide in a creative burst of energy.

The study of grammar is more than the study of the rules and regulations that give order and structure to the language. The study of grammar is the key to the power of words.

CHAPTER 2

PARTS OF SPEECH

Words generate power only when they are crafted into meaningful thoughts. So organized, our words develop the energy to inform, persuade and entertain.

We consider many content and style options as we prepare our messages. In this vital sorting process, we look to many thousands of words that are divided into various compartments. For example, we choose a *verb* for its power and focus. We pick an *adjective* for its color and flair. We select a *pronoun* for its economy. We depend on a *conjunction* to bridge important thoughts.

If we are ignorant of the operating parts of our language and their functions, we cannot create effective thought. We cannot succeed if we do not master the keystone of our language: its organization according to *parts of speech*.

Unfortunately, the term *parts of speech* sometimes evokes nightmarish visions of diagramming sentences and conjugating irregular verbs. This chapter will not perpetuate such an image. We hope it will stimulate you to identify parts of speech and to understand their functions—so that you can harness the power of communication.

What	we	learn	from	parts	of	speech
(pron.)	(pron.)	(verb)	(prep.)	(noun)	(prep.)	(noun)

Let's examine several sentences that illustrate why understanding parts of speech is essential to mastering grammar.

Mixing tacos and puréed tomatoes creates a hearty soup.
(noun—ger.)   (trans. verb—sing.)

This sentence shows how identifying the *-ing* word as a noun and the subject of a sentence helps the writer select the correct number of the verb. *Tacos* and *tomatoes* also are nouns, but *mixing* (the subject) controls verb number. Such an "action" noun is also called a *gerund* (see p. 18).

This is an exciting assignment for us reporters.
(prep.) (pron.—objective case)

By recognizing *for* as a preposition, we select the proper case (objective) for the personal pronoun *we* (us). *Us* is called a *pronoun appositive* (see p. 81) in this sentence and relates to *reporters*.

The disgruntled employee gave Woodstein and me the
(trans. verb)   (indir. obj.)
classified document.

This sentence shows how identification of *verb type* and its *indirect object* helps the writer select the proper case for the personal pronoun (*me*). To write ". . . gave Woodstein and I" would be a serious grammatical error. (See p. 80.)

I feel bad about your spelling test.
(verb) (adj.)

The adjective *bad* describes the subject *I*. That relationship is linked by the verb *feel*. (See p. 15.)

The market <u>plunged</u> <u>badly</u> following a computer-driven sale
          (verb)   (adv.)
of key stocks.

Badly is an adverb, which modifies a verb. It tells to what degree or in what way the market fell. (See p. 25.)

We could cite many other examples to reinforce why we must study parts of speech. Instead, let's look at all eight parts of speech and allow those discussions to make the point themselves.

Traditional grammar texts and courses begin with the noun, following with the pronoun, verb, adjective, adverb, preposition, conjunction and interjection.

Perhaps nouns are mentioned first because of their familiar role as the subject of a sentence. However, such a chronological approach doesn't work in journalism. We look to the heart of the matter—to the power source. That's the *verb,* the major link in a sentence. We'll begin there.

VERBS

Verb may mean "the word" in Latin, but it stands for *power.* A verb is the engine of a sentence; without it, your carefully organized words stand still. A verb indicates *action* or *being.* As such, it is the *only* part of speech that can stand alone as a *complete sentence*.

<u>Wait!</u>

(The subject, *you*, a pronoun, is understood.)

Sentences without strong, convincing verbs lack power and substance. However, verbs don't have to be fancy or complicated. Look at the verb choice in this selection:

They <u>crossed</u> the Hudson ahead of the mail. A fog <u>rolled</u> in at their backs, Manhattan <u>disappeared</u> into the mist like the de-

tail on a fading negative, and the prospect of the West <u>lay</u> before them, a sinful Kodachrome promise.
—Robert Sabbag, "Snow Blind"

These verbs are simple, direct and parallel. "They" didn't *traverse* the river, and the fog didn't *tiptoe* in. Sabbag's verbs were chosen carefully and correctly.

VERB FUNCTIONS

■ **Verbs can state** *action:*

The police officer <u>fired</u> three shots at his assailant.

■ **Verbs can indicate** *being* or *position:*

The suspect <u>was</u> in an alley when police surrounded him.

■ **Verbs can explain a** *state of being:*

The suspect *was* comatose when doctors examined him.

VERB FORMS

The sentences used to illustrate verb functions also show us the three forms of verbs: *transitive, intransitive* and *linking.* Understanding these forms is essential for correct selection of words in a sentence.

1. *Transitive verbs.* In these constructions, the sentence has an *object that receives the action of the verb.* In

The police officer <u>fired</u> three shots at his assailant

the object is *shots,* a noun. Answering the question "Fired what?" gives you a clue to this construction.

Identifying transitive verb forms can help you in *case* selection. In making a *who/whom* choice, for example, focusing on the *object* of the verb makes your task easier:

<u>Whom</u> did you call this morning?

Whom (objective case of *who*) receives the action of the verb *call.* The sentence can also be viewed in this form: You did call *whom* this morning. (Case selection is explained more fully in Chapter 5.)

2. *Intransitive verbs*. These verbs *never* take a direct object; they only show *location* or *being*. In

> The suspect <u>was</u> in an alley when police surrounded him

there is no object following *was;* what follows is just a prepositional phrase. The intransitive verb tells us *where* or *how*, but never *what*.

This sentence also contains an intransitive verb:

> The district attorney <u>collapsed</u> suddenly this morning.

There is no direct action following this verb; what follows is just an amplification of its meaning (*suddenly this morning*). The words following *collapsed* don't answer *what;* they answer *how* and *when*.

Understanding the distinction between transitive and intransitive can prevent frustration in selecting the correct verb from troublesome pairs such as *lay/lie, set/sit* and *raise/rise*. The first verb in these combinations is transitive; it requires an object that answers the question *what*.

> Lay the <u>book</u> on the table.
>
> Have you set your <u>clocks</u> back yet?
>
> Let's raise the <u>roof</u> tonight.
>
> (Objects are underlined.)

On the other hand, verbs such as *lie, sit* and *rise* are intransitive.

> Would you please <u>lie</u> down?
>
> <u>Sit</u> in this chair, please.
>
> I will <u>rise</u> early tomorrow.

It seems simple, but recognizing the distinction between these two sentence constructions—transitive and intransitive—can eliminate most of these verb choice problems.

3. *Linking verbs*. This verb form, which is often a derivative of *to be*, implies a *state of being*. Rather than stating action, this verb connects the subject with a noun, pronoun or adjective to help describe that state of being. See how that "state" is articulated in these sentences:

The <u>suspect</u> <u>was</u> <u>comatose</u> when doctors examined him.
  (subj.) (l. v.)   (adj.)

Before collapsing, the judge complained that <u>he</u> <u>was</u> <u>ill.</u>
                                        (subj.) (l. v.) (adj.)
Have you seen "<u>They</u> <u>Might Be</u> <u>Giants</u>"?
             (subj.)   (l. v.)   (noun)

Although the words following these linking verbs might answer the question *what,* they do not receive any action. Consequently, they are called *predicate nominatives* or *predicate adjectives* because they describe some quality of the subject.

Verbs other than *to be* forms can be linking verbs and indicate a state of being. You can generally substitute *is* for them and make sense of the sentence. They include:

appear	feel	grow	remain	smell	taste
become	get	look	seem	sound	turn

You should note, however, that some verbs can be used in all three verb forms. Whenever reading or writing sentences, be aware of the function of the verbs and surrounding words.

"I <u>smell</u> a rat here," Mayor Thomas told the committee.

(*Transitive* verb—the direct object *rat* follows. *Rat* does not describe a quality of the subject *I.*)

The arson investigator said that some wet rags at the fire scene <u>smelled</u> like kerosene.

(*Intransitive* verb—a prepositional phrase rather than a direct object follows the verb.)

The bullet-riddled corpse <u>smelled</u> bad.

(*Linking* verb—the adjective *bad* follows the verb and describes the state of the corpse.)

Several other aspects of verbs need to be discussed: *principal parts, subjunctive mood* and *verbals.*

PRINCIPAL PARTS OF VERBS

Most of our verbs are *regular;* that is, they form the *past tense* and *past participle* merely by adding *-ed* to the present tense. So, the verb *intend* has these principal parts:

I <u>intend</u> to answer his charges. (present tense)

I <u>intended</u> to be there but was delayed. (past tense)

I <u>have intended</u> to see you for some time. (past participle)

But our language also contains *irregular* verbs, many of which require vowel changes or change of form as their tenses change. Many of these—for example, *ride, rode, ridden* and *break, broke, broken*—are easy to remember. The following is a list of troublesome verbs. Study this list; you may need to refer to it from time to time.

PRESENT	PAST	PAST PARTICIPLE*
begin	began	begun
bring	brought	brought
choose	chose	chosen
dive	dived	dived
drink	drank	drunk
drag	dragged	dragged
drown	drowned	drowned
dye	dyed	dyed
hang (something inanimate)	hung	hung
hang (execution)	hanged	hanged
lay	laid	laid
lead	led	led
lie	lay	lain
plead	pleaded	pleaded
rise	rose	risen
set	set	set
sit	sat	sat
spring	sprang	sprung
wake	woke/waked	waked

*Uses auxiliary verb *has, have* or *had* to form it.

SUBJUNCTIVE MOOD

Occasionally a sentence may be written to express a wish, desire or statement that is *contrary to fact*. The Jewish patriarch Tevye states it well in his song from "Fiddler on the Roof":

If I <u>were</u> a rich man . . . all day long I'd biddy, biddy bum, if I <u>were</u> a wealthy man.

Tevye and his audience understand that he is stating an improbable condition. Hence, he uses the subjunctive *were* instead of *was*.

Although the construction is not as strong, using *auxiliaries* such as *should* or *would* to express conditions or possibilities can help you get around the use of the subjunctive.

If I <u>should</u> ever become rich, I <u>would</u> be a great philanthropist.

VERBALS

What *looks* like a verb, *seems* to have the action of a verb, but is actually a noun or adjective? It is the *verbal* (a gerund, participle or infinitive). Verbals are important to recognize because their improper use can cause you to write incomplete sentences (p. 4) or make errors in parallel structure (p. 68).

1. *Gerunds.* These verbals, which always have an *-ing* form, are often called *verb nouns* because they have the sound of action even when they are the subject of a sentence. Example:

<u>Swimming</u> and <u>weight lifting</u> are wonderful exercises.

(*Swimming* and *weight lifting* are nouns; *are* is the verb.)

Because the gerund always appears in the present participle form of the verb, it is sometimes confused with another verbal, the participle. But as you will see, the participle has a very different use from the gerund.

2. *Participles.* These verbals, which can have an *-ing* or *-ed* form, *are always used as adjectives*. Generally, they modify nouns or pronouns. Examples:

<u>Hoisting</u> her banner proudly, the 78-year-old Sandinista supporter marched confidently toward the capitol.

(*Hoisting* is the present participle form of the verb *hoist* and acts as an *adjective* here, modifying the noun *supporter*.)

<u>Hoisted</u> above the surf by a warm current of air, the intrepid flier guided his hang glider past the dangerous beach cliffs.

(*Hoisted* is the past participle of the verb *hoist* and also acts as an *adjective,* modifying the noun *flier.*)

It should be apparent that the participle as a verbal cannot act as a noun. When a verbal with an *-ing* form modifies a noun or pronoun, it is obviously not a gerund.

3. *Infinitives.* This verbal—*to* plus the present tense of the verb— is the easiest to identify. However, its use is more complicated because an infinitive can function as a noun, adjective or adverb.

> The fiery coach desperately wants <u>to win</u>.

> (In this sentence, the infinitive *to win* is a *noun* because it is the direct object of the transitive verb *wants.*)

> This is the way <u>to win</u>, the fiery coach told her players.

> (The infinitive *to win* in this example is an *adjective* because it modifies the noun *way.* The true verbs in this sentence are *is* and *told.*)

> The fiery coach is eager <u>to win</u>.

> (In this example, the infinitive *to win* is an *adverb* because it modifies the adjective *eager.*)

Nouns

Because it often appears as the subject, the noun has a vital position in the sentence. In referring to a *person, place, thing* or *abstraction* (quality, idea, etc.), the noun has many functions.

Noun Functions

In any sentence the noun can act as:

1. *subject*

> IRS <u>agents</u> seized the files of the investment banker.

2. *direct object* of a transitive verb

> Associated Press reported three traffic <u>deaths</u> this weekend.

3. *predicate nominative* in a linking verb construction

> "He is a <u>charlatan</u>," the witness told the startled jury.

4. *object of a preposition*

Would you deliver this film to the <u>processor</u>?

5. *possessive or modifier*

President <u>Reagan's</u> cabinet nomination hit unexpected opposition in the Senate today. The <u>Reagan</u> cabinet nomination threatens to divide the Senate.

Recognition and correct use of nouns are not serious grammatical problems. However, some writers occasionally have trouble with them in matters of agreement and case.

Perhaps the most common difficulty is with *collective nouns*—words that sound plural but are often singular because of a "one-body" meaning. Words such as *committee, fleet, herd, jury* and *politics* fall into this category.

See Chapter 4 for a discussion of agreement problems and Chapter 5 for a discussion of case.

PRONOUNS

Pronouns often are called "noun substitutes." They help us avoid restating nouns in a sentence, which gives our writing greater flexibility. But they also are more confusing than nouns. Indeed, some of our most common grammar problems relate to pronoun use in matters of case, antecedent agreement, possessives and selection of the proper relative pronoun to introduce a dependent clause. See Chapters 4, 5 and 7.

First, let's review the different types of pronouns: personal, indefinite, relative and interrogative, and demonstrative.

PRONOUN TYPES

1. *Personal.* The most common pronoun type, these pronouns have distinct forms in three cases: nominative, objective and possessive.

NOMINATIVE	OBJECTIVE	POSSESSIVE
I	me	my/mine
you	you	your/yours
he	him	his
she	her	her/hers
it	it	its
we	us	our/ours
you	you	your/yours
they	them	their/theirs

The *personal possessive pronoun* often lures an unnecessary *apostrophe* from the unwary writer. The most common error here relates to *it's*, which is actually a contraction of a pronoun and a verb—*it is*. *Its* (no apostrophe) is the possessive.

It's time for sincere citizen involvement, the candidate said.

(A contraction of *It is time*.)

The runaway dalmatian was returned to its home.

(*Its* modifies *home*.)

Her's, your's and *our's* also are incorrect. Although the apostrophe is used for nouns when forming their possessives (the *car's* engine, *Roosevelt's* third term), the apostrophe is not used with the personal pronoun possessive. These pronouns—his, hers, ours, theirs—are possessives as they stand.

2. *Indefinite.* Pronouns such as *anyone, many, none* and *several* can cause troublesome subject-verb agreement problems because *they show neither person nor number.* The best rule of thumb is to understand the *sense* of the sentence and match the subject and verb in number.

Although the list of indefinite pronouns is long, only three of them can take either a singular or a plural verb, depending on the meaning of the sentence:

all   some   none

Both, few, many and *several* are obviously *plural.*

3. *Relative and interrogative.* Pronouns such as *that, which* and *who* are easy to recognize but sometimes difficult to use properly. The following sentences reflect problems of choice between nominative and objective cases and of the seemingly interchangeable nature of these pronouns:

Who/<u>Whom</u> did you wish to see?

The battleship <u>Missouri</u>, (that/<u>which</u>) is moored in Bremerton, is an awesome spectacle.

This is one of those pens (<u>that</u>/which)(<u>write</u>/writes) under water.

He is the type of leader (that/<u>who</u>) demands unwavering loyalty.

Using these pronouns properly requires an understanding of case, antecedent agreement and restrictive and nonrestrictive clauses. Chapters 3, 4 and 5 deal with these topics. However, this is an appropriate place to mention a common error in the use of the relative pronoun—the use of *that* when *who* is needed. As the next sentence illustrates, the use of *that* to avoid a *who/whom* selection is poor grammar.

The police officers <u>that</u> stopped my car were polite but firm.

Who, not *that,* is needed when the antecedent (in this case, *officers*) is human or takes on personal human qualities.

Who has a separate possessive form. The previous warning about unnecessary contractions also applies here; don't write *who's* (*who is*) when you mean *whose.*

Alice Franklin, 89, <u>whose</u> Social Security money was stolen this afternoon when she was knocked to the pavement by neighborhood toughs, discovered tonight that she has many friends <u>who</u> care.

(Note also the use of the relative pronoun *who* instead of *that.*)

4. *Demonstrative.* These include pronouns like *this, that, these* and *those.* They are pronouns as long as they function as true noun substitutes—that is, as long as they function as subjects, objects and objects of prepositions. Hence, in the sentence,

<u>This</u> is exactly what I mean

this serves as the subject of the sentence. The distinction needs to be made because the same four pronouns can also be adjectives if they are used to modify other words, such as nouns (*this chair, that desk,* etc.).

ADJECTIVES

Writers are counseled to select strong, direct verbs to lay a proper foundation for the sentence. Although this is important, not far behind is the need to select appropriate and creative adjectives.

Adjectives describe, limit and qualify nouns and pronouns. (They do not modify verbs; that is the realm of the adverb.) Adjectives are picture words; they enhance the framework of a sentence. As Roget's Thesaurus indicates, there are numerous adjectives, and that makes their selection difficult. Given their many nuances, adjectives challenge the writer to be on target with meanings.

TYPES OF ADJECTIVES

1. *Descriptive.* These adjectives paint more *detail* into the picture. They also set a *mood.* Note this section of a well-written story about the crash of a commuter plane (descriptive adjectives underlined):

> OWL'S HEAD, Maine—The pilot's cap was <u>crushed</u> and <u>muddied</u>. His headset was <u>bent</u> and <u>broken</u>. A woman's <u>delicate</u>, <u>purple</u> scarf hung from a <u>jagged</u> piece of metal. <u>Crumpled</u> and <u>bloodstained</u> maps hung from where the nose of the plane should have been. <u>Green</u> body bags were filled with corpses. . . .
>
> In the <u>tangled</u> jumble of an airplane crash, there is no reason. . . .
> —The Boston Globe

Careful writers are concerned more with content than with flashiness. For them, a simple yet precise adjective provides the best description of all.

2. *Limiting.* Whereas the descriptive adjective stresses things artistic and colorful, the limiting adjective is more spartan. In blue jeans parlance, the descriptive adjective has a designer label, but the limiting adjective is plain pockets. It sets boundaries and qualifies meanings.

The lost hunters hiked 12 miles to reach help.

(The number *12* gives us a no-nonsense view of how much hiking the hunters had to do. The miles are not described as tortuous or snow-clogged. Choosing a limiting modifier, the writer merely wants to give us an exact view.)

"This fumble cost us the game," the coach said sadly.

(We can see how a specific fumble turned the fortunes of the team. Although *this* is a limiting adjective here, *this, these* and *those* may also be known as *demonstrative adjectives* when they modify nouns.)

Whose feature photograph will win the Pulitzer this year?

(There are two limiting adjectives in this sentence: *whose*, which is also called an *interrogative adjective*, and *this*, which also could be called *demonstrative*.)

Do you know any ways to improve your writing?

(In a sense, the adjective *any* is limiting in that it sets boundaries—extremely wide ones—but does not describe them. For this reason, adjectives such as *any, each* and *either* are often called *indefinite adjectives* when they modify a noun.)

THE PREDICATE ADJECTIVE

An adjective can also follow a linking verb and modify the subject of the sentence. In this form it is called a *predicate adjective* because its relationship to the subject is transmitted through the verb. (Hence the idea of "linking.")

Because the smoke detectors were defective, the fire blazed for two hours before it was discovered.

(*Defective* is the predicate adjective because it modifies *detectors*. Read it as "defective detectors," and you can see this relationship better. In this way, you can also see that the verb is *linking* rather than *transitive*.)

Wine reviewers reported that the Chablis was too acidic.

(Read this relationship as *acidic Chablis*.)

VERBALS AS ADJECTIVES

Two verbals, the participle and the infinitive, can be classified as adjectives. Whereas the participle is always an adjective, the infinitive is an adjective only when it modifies a noun. (Infinitives can also be a noun or adverb.)

<u>Swimming</u> with the carefree abandon of a schoolboy in summer, he reached the raft in the middle of the lake.

(*Swimming* modifies the pronoun *he*.)

The senator announced a plan <u>to combat</u> the trade deficit.

(The infinitive *to combat* modifies the noun *plan*.)

DEGREES OF ADJECTIVES

Many adjectives and adverbs have three forms that reflect *degrees of intensity* or *comparison*. For example,

high   higher   highest

reflect a movement from the base word *high* to the comparative level *higher* (than something else) to the superlative level (*highest*) at which no comparison can be made.

Although some words take an *-er* or *-est* to show a change in degree, others retain their base form and just add *more* or *most* to show this change:

skilled   more skilled   most skilled

It is important to check that your comparisons make sense and that you do not restate the superlative degree for words that are already superlative in their meaning. (See a further discussion of this in "Comparatives and Superlatives" in the following section on adverbs.)

ADVERBS

Although adverbs perform descriptive and limiting functions like adjectives, they are sometimes more difficult to identify in a sentence. But like the adjective, the adverb can be easily overused.

It is not enough to know that an adverb can modify a verb, an adjective or another adverb, or that many adverb forms end in *-ly*. Adverbs also can introduce sentences, connect independent clauses, modify entire phrases or sentences and state *degree, time* and *manner:*

> The paramedics drove <u>hurriedly</u> to the accident scene.
>
> (The adverb *hurriedly* modifies the verb *drove;* it answers "how.")
>
> He is <u>quite</u> handsome, don't you agree?
>
> (*Quite* modifies the adjective *handsome;* it states the degree.)
>
> The prime minister took her defeat <u>very</u> badly.
>
> (*Very* modifies the adverb *badly,* which modifies the verb *took.*)
>
> <u>Why</u> are you calling me at 4 a.m.?
>
> (This interrogative adverb modifies the verb *are calling;* it shows purpose.)
>
> The prime rate of interest may fall soon; <u>however</u>, it should not have a profound effect on employment.
>
> (*However* connects two independent clauses; in this form, it is called a *conjunctive adverb.*)

Although writers are cautioned to select only the most appropriate and descriptive of adverbs, they also should be concerned about where to position them in a sentence. Some people mistake adverbs for adjectives because of the adverb's mobility in a sentence. One reason to move an adverb is to improve *emphasis.* However, writers must position adverbs as close to the words they intend to modify, or confusion could result:

> <u>Only</u> I love you.
>
> I love you <u>only</u>.

COMPARATIVES AND SUPERLATIVES

The adverbial comparative indicates a comparison between two units, and its superlative indicates the highest degree of quality among three or more units. Examples:

> The Lotus accelerated <u>more quickly</u> than all of the formula racers on the track today. (comparative)
>
> The Lotus accelerates the <u>most quickly</u> of all the formula racers manufactured today. (superlative—no higher degree)

When using the comparative, writers should ensure that their meaning is clear. Examples:

Hypertension is decidedly more pernicious than any chronic disease in America today.

(In this reading, hypertension is also more pernicious than itself, because it is a chronic disease too. The remainder of the sentence should read: "than any *other* chronic disease in America today.")

This has to be the most supreme example of ignorance I have ever encountered.

(Certain words, called *absolutes*, defy comparisons. By definition, *supreme* is already superlative. Other common absolutes are *perfect, excellent, impossible, final* and *unique*.)

The previous example is easily corrected:

This has to be as supreme an example of ignorance as I have ever encountered.

As we stated before, degrees of comparison also apply to adjectives.

PREPOSITIONS

They may not seem very exotic, but prepositions have important functions in a sentence. They use nouns and pronouns to create phrases, and they link these phrases to the rest of the sentence.

Like many other parts of speech, prepositions can have highly specific meanings. Writers are sometimes confused about the correct choice in such pairs as *between/among, beside/besides, because of/ due to, on/upon* and *beneath/below.* A good writer will become aware of the intended meanings of these prepositions.

The prepositions we use most frequently include:

at   by   for   from   in   of   on   to   with

Here is a list of the simple and compound prepositions that are used less frequently:

aboard	among	beyond	in spite	since§
about	around	but†	of	through
above	as far as*	concerning	like‡	throughout
according	because of	contrary to	near	toward
to	before	despite	next to	under
across	behind	down	out of	until
after	beside	during	over	upon
against	besides	inside	past	within
ahead of	between	into	per	without
along				

---

*Not a preposition if used as an introductory phrase.
†Meaning *except*.
‡Often mistaken for a conjunction and used incorrectly to link clauses.
§Can also be a conjunction and an adverb.

Prepositional phrases (a preposition followed by a noun or pronoun) modify verbs, nouns and adjectives in a sentence. No matter what they modify, these phrases require the objective case for the noun or pronoun that is the object of the preposition. So, it would not be proper to write

This death threat was meant <u>for</u> you and <u>I</u>.

For is a common preposition, so it should be obvious that *you and me* should serve as its object. Prepositional phrases always have objects; even more than 300 years ago, the English poet John Donne never would have considered the phrase "for *who* the bell tolls." He wrote, of course, "never send to know for *whom* the bell tolls; it tolls for thee." For more discussion of case, see Chapter 5.

Grammarians have concerns about the excessive use of prepositions in a sentence. Some compound prepositions, such as *with reference to, on account of* and *in connection with* can hurt the clarity of a sentence; indeed, your sentence may not need a prepositional phrase at all. Inspect it. See Chapter 9 on clarity and conciseness for examples.

One final point about prepositions: Can you place them at the end of a sentence? We feel the same way about this as we do about cracking open fresh eggs with only one hand. *Do it as long as you don't make a mess.* Scrambling a sentence in order to put a preposition in the center of it often creates an awkward construction. Example:

This is a sentence up with which a writer will not put.

You're looking for clarity, right? Isn't that what good writing is *about?*

CONJUNCTIONS

Some cynics believe that the presence of a conjunction in a sentence means the construction is going to be long and complex—that is, it will be so long that the conjunction will be needed to bridge it. They're right about the linking function of the conjunction, but they're off target in their prediction of what comes with it. In fact, a conjunction can help maintain the rhythm and coherence of a sentence, as well as provide needed transitions.

A conjunction frequently joins whole clauses. It does this in two ways.

COORDINATING AND SUBORDINATING CONJUNCTIONS

In the first way, a conjunction *coordinates* two clauses of *equal* grammatical weight. Generally this occurs with two independent clauses (those that could stand as separate, complete sentences if they were not joined). Example:

> Council members approved the anti-nudity ordinance, <u>but</u> they defeated the gun control measure.

The conjunction *but* links the two equal portions of the sentence. Conjunctions can also link simple words and phrases.

> I enjoy baseball <u>and</u> foot reflexology.

> He jumped out of the frying pan <u>and</u> into the fire.

In a second way, a conjunction can join clauses of *unequal* weight. It is called *subordinating,* because it connects an independent or main clause with a subordinate or dependent clause (a clause that would not be a complete sentence if separated from the rest of the construction).

<u>Unless</u> the voters approve a $6.8 million operating levy to-day, the Estacada School District will be forced to close its doors.

(The conjunction introduces the subordinate clause and links it to the main clause.)

Here are lists of the common coordinating and subordinating conjunctions.

COORDINATING		SUBORDINATING			
and	or	after	before	so	when
but	yet	although	how	through	where
for	while	as	if	unless	while
nor		as if	since		

Note the subordinating conjunction *as if.* Be wary of substitutes; *like*, a preposition, is often used improperly:

It looks <u>like</u> it will rain today.

Remember that prepositions take objects and create phrases with them. They do not link clauses, such as "it will rain today." A writer has two choices here:

◻ to use a subordinating conjunction properly

It looks <u>as if</u> it will rain today.

◻ to give the preposition its simple object

It looks like <u>rain</u> today.

CORRELATIVE CONJUNCTIONS

Another class of conjunctions works only in pairs. They are called *correlative,* because they pair words, phrases and clauses to provide balance.

The seminar was <u>both</u> stimulating <u>and</u> relaxing.

<u>Neither</u> the players <u>nor</u> the coach was indicted.*

Other common correlative conjunctions are *either . . . or, not only . . . but also,* and *whether . . . or.*

---

*If the singular verb in this construction seems odd, see p. 61.

ADVERBS THAT LOOK LIKE
CONJUNCTIONS

Certain words that seem to have conjunctive qualities actually are adverbs. Words such as *accordingly, consequently, however, moreover, nevertheless* and *therefore* are sometimes inserted between two *independent* clauses for transition. For this reason, they are called *conjunctive adverbs*.

> This meeting lacks a quorum; therefore, I will adjourn it until next Wednesday.

> (Note that these two clauses cannot be joined by a comma; the semicolon tells you that the link word therefore is being used adverbially.)

INTERJECTIONS

After such a long hike through parts of speech, it is delightful to encounter the clean and simple outpost known as the *interjection*. Also called the *exclamation,* the interjection gives emotion and outburst to a sentence. It often stands alone and has its own punctuation.

> Whew! Four hours in a sauna is too much for me.

Occasionally an interjection is included in a sentence:

> Oh, give me strength!

Note, however, that a sentence may have an exclamation mark in it but not contain an interjection.

Journalists rarely use an interjection in conventional news stories unless it appears in direct quotations. This part of speech obviously carries a strong editorial voice, but even textbook authors succumb to its use sometimes:

> Yippee! We're glad this chapter is done!
> (Aren't you?)

CHAPTER 3

THE SENTENCE

We are born knowing how to make sentences.

Linguist Noam Chomsky and biologist Lewis Thomas tell us that humans are genetically programmed to identify grammatical patterns. "The capacity . . . to organize and deploy words into intelligible sentences," writes Thomas, "is innate in the human mind."

When our brains buzz with definitions, exceptions, procedures and regulations, it is easy to forget that most of us have been speaking in logical sentences since we were 18 months old. When we study the parts, types and pitfalls of sentences, let's remember that we are investigating a subject that just may be at the core of being human.

On, then, to an old friend: the sentence. A *sentence* is a

self-contained grammatical unit that ends with a "full-stop" punctuation mark (period, question mark or exclamation point). It must contain a verb and a subject (stated or implied), and it must state a complete thought.

A sentence can be as concise as a single word: *Go. Wait. Stop.* (The subject *you* is implied.) It can be as expansive as one of William Faulkner's 100-word constructions. Regardless of length, grammatically correct sentences result from the same procedure: the selection, manipulation and coordination of sentence parts.

SENTENCE PARTS

PREDICATES AND SUBJECTS

A sentence can be divided into two parts: the *predicate* and the *subject.*

The *simple predicate* of a sentence is the verb. The *simple subject* is the noun or noun substitute.

> The <u>audience</u> <u>applauded.</u>
>   (simp.   (simp.
>   subj.)   pred.)

The *complete predicate* includes the verb plus all its complements and modifiers. The *complete subject* includes the noun or noun substitute and all its complements and modifiers. In the following sentence the complete predicate is the verb plus its adverb; the complete subject is the noun plus its modifiers:

> The middle-aged <u>audience</u> <u>applauded loudly.</u>
>   (complete subj.)   (complete pred.)

We can continue to describe and modify both the subject and the predicate parts of the sentence:

> The standing-room-only, middle-aged <u>audience</u> <u>applauded</u>
>   (complete subj.)   (complete
> <u>wildly, hooting, stamping feet and throwing hats in the air.</u>
>   pred.)

In addition to modifiers and descriptive phrases, action verbs can be complemented by direct objects, indirect objects and prepositional phrases, all of which are considered part of the predicate. A *direct object* is any noun or noun substitute that answers the question *what* or *whom*. An *indirect object* tells *to whom* or *for what* the action is done. A *prepositional phrase* is a preposition followed by its object. Because these complements must be in the objective case, recognizing them will help you avoid making errors in case.

The audience applauded <u>the performer</u>.
(dir. obj.)

The audience applauded <u>her</u>.
(dir. obj.,
objective case)

The audience gave <u>the performer</u> a <u>standing ovation</u>.
(indir. obj.)   (dir. obj.)

The audience gave <u>him</u> a standing ovation.
(indir. obj.,
objective case)

The audience tossed rotten fruit <u>at the yodeling acrobats</u>.
(prep. phrase)

The audience tossed rotten fruit at <u>them</u>.
(obj. of prep.,
objective case)

The complement of a linking verb is a noun or adjective describing the subject. These words are also considered part of the predicate.

The performer is an <u>amateur</u>.
(pred. noun)
The audience seems <u>rude</u>.
(pred. adj.)

PHRASES AND CLAUSES

When we construct sentences, we use phrases and clauses as building blocks. A *phrase* is a group of related words that lacks both a subject and a predicate. Phrases come in two basic varieties: *prepositional phrases* (a preposition followed by its object) and *verbal phrases* (a form of the verb—infinitive, gerund or participle—that does not act as a verb, accompanied by its object or related material).

The recent hepatitis outbreak was the first <u>in more than 10 years.</u> (prep. phrase)

<u>To stop the disease from spreading</u> was the first priority. (inf. phrase)

<u>Tracing the source of the disease</u> didn't take health officials long. (ger. phrase)

(The gerund phrase acts as a noun.)

<u>Following a lead</u>, they zeroed in on Curry-in-a-Hurry, a (pres. part. phrase) downtown restaurant.

(The participle phrase acts as an adjective modifying *they*.)

<u>Infected with the virus</u>, one restaurant employee was found (past part. phrase) responsible for spreading the disease to 300 patrons.

(The participle phrase acts as an adjective modifying <u>employee</u>.)

Recognizing phrases and knowing what functions they perform in a sentence can help you in at least two ways. First, you will never try to construct a sentence simply by ending a phrase with a "full-stop" punctuation mark. Because a phrase does not include a subject or a predicate, it cannot act as a sentence. What it is, as we will see later in this chapter, is a *fragment.* Second, you will avoid misplacing a participle phrase because you recognize that it modifies a noun and must be placed as close as possible to that noun. (For a discussion of misplaced modifiers, see Chapter 9.)

A *clause* is a group of related words that contains a subject and predicate. An *independent* or *main clause* is a complete sentence.

Mountain rescue workers found the stranded skiers.

A *dependent* or *subordinate clause,* although it also contains a subject and predicate, does not express a complete thought. It is not a sentence and cannot stand alone. To become a grammatical sentence, it must be linked to a main clause.

After they spotted a flare.
(dep. clause)

After they spotted a flare, **mountain rescue workers found**
(dep. clause linked with main clause)
the stranded skiers.

Dependent clauses come in three varieties according to the function they perform in a sentence. A *noun clause* takes the place of a noun or a noun substitute; an *adjective clause* serves as an adjective; an *adverb clause* acts as an adverb.

That mountain rescue workers found the stranded skiers
was no surprise.   (noun clause)

(It, a pronoun, can be substituted for the clause.)

The rescue workers, **who were all specially trained,** **found**
(adj. clause)
the stranded skiers. (The clause modifies the noun *workers*.)

After they crossed the glacier, **the mountain rescue**
(adv. clause)
workers found the skiers.

(The clause modifies the verb by answering when.)

Recognizing dependent clauses is important. Not only will you avoid using them as sentences—the fragment error—but also you can learn to use these clauses to add variety to the structure of your sentences.

TYPES OF SENTENCES

Sentences come in four varieties according to the number and type of clauses they contain.

Simple Sentences

A *simple sentence* contains one independent clause. The most common construction is subject-verb-object.

Forecasters predicted rain.
  (subj.)   (verb)   (obj.)

We can add modifiers—single words or phrases—but regardless of the number of words, the sentence remains *simple* if it contains a single clause.

National forecasters today predicted more rain
(adj.)   (adv.)   (adj.)
for the coast, valley and interior regions.
                    (prep. phrase)

Compound Sentences

A *compound sentence* has two or more independent (main) clauses, each containing a subject and predicate and each expressing a complete thought. The two complete clauses, equal or nearly equal in importance, are linked (coordinated) by a conjunction and a comma, semicolon or colon. *And, but, or, nor* and *yet* are the conjunctions, sometimes referred to as *coordinating connectives*.

The river has reached flood stage, and thousands of
      (indep. clause)   (conj.)   (indep.
residents may be in danger.
    clause)

The river has reached flood stage; thousands of residents
      (indep. clause)   (indep.
may be in danger.
    clause)

The river has reached flood stage, and one thing is certain:
      (indep. clause)   (indep. clause)
Thousands of residents will be in danger.
      (indep. clause)

Punctuation is probably the most common problem associated with compound sentences. Because the two (or more) clauses are independent—actually complete sentences on their own—they cannot be linked with a comma alone. The comma is a brief pause used to separate phrases or dependent clauses from the kernel of the sentence. By itself, it is too weak a punctuation mark to separate complete thoughts. You should use both a comma and a coordinating conjunction. If you omit the coordinating conjunction, use a semicolon, or occasionally a colon. We will discuss this further in "Run-on Sentences" later in this chapter and in Chapter 7, which discusses punctuation.

COMPLEX SENTENCES

A *complex sentence* contains one independent (main) clause and at least one dependent (subordinate) clause. The subordinate clause depends on the main clause for both meaning and grammatical completion.

> Because mortgage rates are low, the housing industry is
>   (dep. clause)   (indep.
> flourishing.
>   clause)

> The housing industry will flourish as long as mortgage rates
>   (indep. clause)   (dep.
> continue to remain low.
>   clause)

In the two preceding complex sentences, conjunctions (*because, as long as*) introduce the dependent clauses. These words, sometimes called *subordinating connectives,* establish the relationship between the two sentence parts. Our language has a variety of conjunctions, each with its own precise meaning. The careful writer chooses the subordinating conjunction that best expresses the specific relationship between the dependent and the independent clause. For example:

RELATIONSHIP	CONJUNCTIONS
cause and effect	because, due to, as a result of, if
sequence	after, before, during, while
time, place	when, whenever, since, where, until, as long as

A dependent clause can also be subordinated to the main clauses by relative pronouns: *who, whom, whose, which* or *that*. Note in the first of the following examples that the main clause can be interrupted by the dependent clause.

> The senator <u>who took the bribe</u> was re-elected.
> (dep. clause)
>
> The state legislature vetoed a bill <u>that would drastically cut</u>
> (dep.
> <u>funding for higher education.</u>
> clause)

COMPOUND-COMPLEX SENTENCES

A *compound-complex* sentence contains at least two main clauses and one dependent clause. This construction seems to invite wordiness, but a careful writer will refuse to fall into the trap. The following three-clause sentence is concise:

> <u>Although the river flooded,</u> <u>no one was injured,</u> and
> (dep. clause)   (indep. clause)
> <u>no property was damaged.</u>
> (indep. clause)

But the compound-complex sentence can also be a monster:

> <u>Because of changes in the county land-use planning policy</u>
> (dep.
> <u>that the state agency mandated last week,</u> <u>Monroe</u>
> clause)   (indep.
> <u>County commissioners will have to devise a new compre-</u>
> clause)
> <u>hensive development plan,</u> and <u>west county residents will</u>
> (indep.
> <u>gain control over 1,000 acres of prime agricultural land.</u>
> clause)

The preceding sentence rambles along a confused route of one dependent and two independent clauses. A newspaper reader would lose interest. A broadcaster would gasp for breath. Many a compound-complex sentence would be better off as two reconstructed sentences. For example:

Because of changes in the county land-use planning policy, Monroe County commissioners will have to devise a new comprehensive development plan. The changes, mandated by the state agency last week, mean west county residents will gain control over 1,000 acres of prime agricultural land.

A GOOD SENTENCE

It says precisely what you want it to say. You begin by choosing words carefully, respectful of their meanings and aware of their sounds and rhythms. Then you form the words into clusters and join the clusters with invisible seams. A pattern emerges. It has grammatical unity. The idea is coherent, the statement concise. You sit back to marvel.

You have written a good sentence.

SENTENCE ERRORS

Perhaps you haven't written a good sentence. Maybe you've fallen prey to one of the following ungrammatical or sluggish constructions: a sentence fragment, a run-on sentence, oversubordination or dead construction.

SENTENCE FRAGMENTS

A fragment is literally a broken piece. It is a group of words sheared off from or never attached to the sentence. The group of words may lack a subject, a predicate, a complete thought or any combination of the three. No matter what it lacks, it is not a grammatical sentence. It cannot stand alone. If you punctuate it as if it were a sentence, you have created a fragment.

Like this one.

Fragments can be single words, brief phrases or lengthy dependent clauses. The number of words is irrelevant. What matters is that the words do not meet the definition of a sentence. A common mistake is to look only for subject and verb and, having found them, to believe you have written a complete sentence. Remember, a sentence expresses a complete thought.

Although he announced his candidacy

contains a subject *(he)* and a verb *(announced)* but does not express a complete thought. It is a dependent clause, a fragment.

He announced his candidacy. (complete sentence)

Although he announced his candidacy, he said he had no chance of winning. (complete sentence)

CORRECTING FRAGMENTS

Now that you know what a sentence is and what parts it must contain, avoiding fragments should not be difficult. First, recognize the fragment. It can be a single word, a phrase or a dependent clause. Now you have three choices: Rewrite the fragment to include a subject, verb and complete thought; incorporate the fragment into a complete sentence; add to the fragment, making it a complete sentence.

The state Public Health Council has adopted new, stringent smoking regulations. No smoking in malls.

(fragment underlined)

The state Public Health Council has adopted new, stringent smoking regulations. No smoking will be permitted in malls.

(fragment rewritten as complete thought)

The state Public Health Council has adopted new, stringent smoking regulations, including a ban on smoking in malls.

(fragment incorporated into complete sentence)

The state Public Health Council has adopted new, stringent smoking regulations. The no-smoking-in-malls rule may be particularly controversial.

(additions to fragment to form complete sentence)

Feature writers, speech writers and advertising copywriters will tell you that fragments can serve a useful purpose. In appropriate instances, to achieve particular effects, certain grammatical rules can be broken. But accidental fragments are a grammatical error. *Purposeful fragments*—consistent with the subject, the audience and the medium—are a matter of style.

RUN-ON SENTENCES

A run-on sentence doesn't know when to quit. Rushing forward without proper punctuation, this construction may actually carry with it two or three sentences.

> County finances are in trouble, voters once again defeated a property tax increase.

This sentence is actually two independent clauses run together with a comma. Using commas to link independent clauses (without the help of a conjunction) almost always results in a run-on sentence. In fact this "comma-splice" error is the most common cause of run-on sentences. But if you can recognize an independent clause and if you understand the limitations of the comma, you can avoid the error.

The most frequently used of all punctuation marks, the comma serves a variety of purposes: separating clauses linked by conjunctions, separating items in a series, setting off introductory phrases, setting off nonrestrictive clauses or appositives, and avoiding ambiguity. But one job a comma rarely performs is creating a long pause between independent clauses. This function is performed by either the semicolon or the period. When you force the comma to do a job for which it is not designed, you create a grammatically incorrect construction.

Rarely, and only with extreme care, a writer might violate the comma-splice rule. When a sentence is composed of three or more brief parallel (in both construction and idea) clauses, commas might be used.

> Be correct, be concise, be coherent.

In certain kinds of writing—a stylistic feature story, for example—a writer might purposefully create comma-splice run-on sentences to achieve a particular effect. But this kind of rule breaking depends on knowing and respecting the rule.

Comma-splice run-ons, in addition to being grammatically incorrect, almost always lack coherence. A comma signals readers that they are reading one continuous idea interrupted by a brief pause (the comma). Readers expect the words following a comma to augment or complement what they have just read. But in a comma-splice run-on, the sense of the sentence (actually two or more whole, complete thoughts) denies the message of the comma. There is not one continuous idea. New thoughts are introduced without the benefit of connections between the thoughts (for example, *but, and, or*).

Writers also create run-ons when they fuse two or more complete sentences without any punctuation:

> County finances are in trouble voters once again defeated a property tax increase.

Another error to watch out for is the inappropriate use of *and.* When you use *and* to link two independent clauses, you are telling the reader that the two thoughts either reinforce the same point or follow each other "as they happen." *And* does not express a specific relationship between the two sentences; it merely coordinates them. If you link two complete ideas that neither reinforce each other nor follow one another in sequence, you create a rambling sentence.

> The county faces budget problems, and the voters once again defeated a property tax increase.

This error is often called *excessive coordination* (*and* is a coordinating conjunction), but the resulting sentence looks much like a run-on and can be corrected in the same way you correct run-ons.

CORRECTING RUN-ONS

You can correct a run-on sentence four ways:

1. Change the run-on sentence into two (or more) complete sentences. Add periods and capital letters.

County finances are in trouble. Voters once again defeated a property tax increase.

2. If there is a close relationship between the two (or more) complete thoughts (clauses) in the run-on, insert a semicolon between them to express this relationship. A semicolon shows this connection and allows the reader to move swiftly from the first sentence to the second.

County finances are in trouble; voters once again defeated a property tax increase.

3. In a comma-splice run-on, connect the two sentences with a coordinating conjunction if the two parts are of equal weight. Use *and, but, or, nor, yet* or *so* according to the meaning of the sentence. Always use a comma before the conjunction.

County finances are in trouble, yet voters once again defeated the property tax increase.

4. If the relationship between the two (or more) independent clauses is such that one clause depends on the other, rewrite the "dependent" sentence as a dependent clause and place it in front of or after the main (independent) clause. To do this, choose a subordinating conjunction that expresses the nature of the dependent relationship and place it in front of the appropriate sentence. Subordinating conjunctions include *after, because, while, when, where, since, if* and *although.*

Although county finances are in trouble, voters once again defeated a property tax increase.

County finances are in trouble because voters once again defeated a property tax increase.

OVERSUBORDINATED SENTENCES

Subordination, the fourth of the ways just listed to correct a run-on sentence, is the technique of making one idea less important than, or subordinate to, another. Consider these sentences:

Rita Falk won the match.

Rita Falk was suffering from tendinitis.

Assuming the idea in the first sentence is the more important one, you can subordinate the idea in the second sentence by creating a dependent clause and attaching it to the main sentence.

Although Rita Falk was suffering from tendinitis, she won the match.

Rita Falk, who was suffering from tendinitis, won the match.

Subordinating one idea to another—creating complex sentences—is a useful sentence-building technique. But beware of oversubordination.

A string of dependent clauses, or one excessively long dependent clause, placed before the main sentence can slow the pace. You make your audience wait too long to get to the important idea, and you risk losing and confusing them.

When she was only 17, while suffering from tendinitis, Rita Falk won the match. (oversubordination)

Rita Falk, 17, won the match although she was suffering from tendinitis. (improved)

Although she suffered from tendinitis, which seemed to diminish the power of her stroke and slow her movement on the court, Rita Falk won the match. (lengthy introductory clause)

Rita Falk won the match despite the tendinitis, which seemed to diminish the power of her stroke and slow her movement on the court. (main clause first)

Another type of oversubordination occurs when several dependent clauses are tacked on to the end of the main clause. The result is a confusing succession of modifiers.

Rita Falk beat Lynne Galloway, who was then undefeated, who double-faulted her first three serves while the crowd watched in disbelief. (tacked-on clauses)

Rita Falk beat the undefeated Lynne Galloway. Galloway double-faulted her first three serves as the crowd watched in disbelief. (improved)

You can also get into subordination trouble when you begin a sentence with a dependent clause, move to the main clause and then add a second dependent clause that attempts to modify the meaning of the first. The result is an awkward, confusing sentence.

Because she won the match, Rita Falk will advance to the finals, **although she suffered from tendinitis.**

(front and back subordination)

Winning the match despite tendinitis, Rita Falk will advance to the finals. (improved)

DEAD CONSTRUCTIONS

Perhaps they are holdovers from term paper writing style, but these constructions have little place in journalistic writing: *it is* and *there is*. In most cases, these words, called *expletives,* merely take up space, performing no function in the sentence. Not only do they add clutter, but they often rob the sentence of its power by shifting emphasis from what could be a strong verb to a weaker construction—a linking verb (*is, was* and other forms of *to be*).

There was a **march** by 2,000 anti-apartheid demonstrators today. (verb potential)

Two thousand anti-apartheid demonstrators **marched** today.

It is the students' **plan** to force the university to divest its funds. (verb potential)

The students **plan** to force the university to divest its funds.

In addition to strengthening the sentence by using an action verb, avoiding *there is/there are* constructions has another benefit: simpler subject-verb agreement. *There* is not usually a subject. Whether you use *is* or *are* depends on what follows the verb.

There **is** a **law** against smoking in public places.
There **are** **plans** to enforce it.

Looking for the subject after the verb often creates agreement confusion. Avoid both the confusion and the dead construction by restructuring the sentences.

Smoking in public places is against the law. (or illegal)

The city plans to enforce the law.

It is/there is constructions are not entirely without value. You might purposefully choose this structure to add emphasis to the subject.

It was the new senator who cast the deciding vote. (emphasis)

The new senator cast the deciding vote. (no emphasis)

A good rule to follow is this: If *it is/there is* merely takes up space in the sentence, restructure the sentence. Rescue the "hidden verb" and avoid agreement problems. If on occasion you want to emphasize the subject, use *it is/there is,* but use it sparingly.

THE LEAD SENTENCE

Whether they write news, features, columns or editorials, whether they work for newspapers, magazines, radio or TV, journalists agree on one thing: *The first sentence is the most important one in the story.*

In traditional news style (the "inverted pyramid" structure), the first sentence is designed to give the reader, listener or viewer a concise, comprehensive summary of the most important elements of the story. Journalists must combine their news sense and their language skills to write this lead sentence. Not only is it the first sentence their audience reads or hears, but it may also be the *only* sentence. Demands on time, distractions in the environment or just plain lack of interest mean that news consumers frequently stop reading or listening after the lead sentence. For the journalist this translates into a heavy burden: Either you inform your audience immediately or you don't inform them at all.

News sense, of course, comes first. A journalist must learn to recognize what elements of the story are most newsworthy, what facts matter most to the audience. But inextricably tied to this is the journalist's ability to express these "lead elements" in direct, concise and grammatically correct language.

You often have to pack a great deal of information into a summary lead sentence. This "packing" increases the chances you may write a muddled, rambling or otherwise awkward sentence. Run-ons and oversubordination are frequent problems because you have much information to include.

> State lawmakers failed to resolve a budget-balancing stalemate, they worked all week but had to recess for the weekend Friday night. (run-on)

> After failing to resolve a budget-balancing stalemate, even though they worked all week, state lawmakers recessed for the weekend Friday night. (oversubordination)

> After failing in a week-long attempt to resolve the budget-balancing stalemate, state lawmakers recessed for the weekend Friday night. (improved)

Writing a simple lead sentence with subject–verb–object construction is sometimes difficult because of the amount of information you must include. Remember that compound and complex sentences, if constructed economically, can be both clear and concise.

> The student body president announced her resignation, and the senate voted to disband three committees at a free-for-all meeting last night. (compound lead sentence)

> The Board of Education voted last night to allow the distribution of birth control information in district high schools after health officials presented disturbing new data on teenage pregnancy. (complex lead sentence)

In general, however, avoid compound-complex lead sentences. They make your audience work too hard for the meaning.

The summary sentence is not the only kind of lead journalists write. The other major category might be called the *attention grabber*. Here journalists do not attempt to present the most important story elements. Instead, they try to entice the audience. This is no place for oversubordinated sentences or dead construction. Lean and strong sentences are a necessity.

He is the most misunderstood man in Chicago.

On the battlefield of failing businesses, Jane Jones shoots the wounded.

Paul Hansen says he was only trying to help.

Of course all sentences should be constructed both grammatically and gracefully. The lead, however, deserves particular attention.

THE TRANSITIONAL SENTENCE

Another important sentence in journalistic writing—whatever the style, whatever the medium—is the transitional sentence. Transitions are essential to the coherence of a story. They move the reader or listener from idea to idea by stating or implying the connection between ideas.

In a story, transitions act as both glue and grease. By expressing or implying the relationship between sentences, paragraphs or sections of a story, transitions fasten story elements. They help create flow and direction in a story. They keep the story moving, logically and coherently, and keep the audience attentive.

TRANSITIONAL WORDS

Creating a sentence that links one idea to another often means beginning that sentence with a transitional word or phrase or using a transitional word to link ideas within the sentence. In the following example, transitional words both between and within sentences are underlined.

Steelworkers in West Virginia are negotiating the purchase of one of the biggest mills in the state. Most workers and townspeople are backing the plan, <u>but</u> some union officials have reservations.

    <u>Because</u> the current plan would mean a 30 percent reduction in salary and benefits for the steelworkers, top union officials say the negotiations are far from over. <u>However</u>, they realize failure to reach some agreement will result in permanent closure of the mill <u>and</u> unemployment for 7,000 workers.

    <u>Indeed</u>, officials say they are bending over backward to negotiate with the Standard Steel Co., owners of the mill. <u>Similarly</u>, government officials in this company town say they are prepared to make certain concessions.

Our language has a variety of words to express different relationships between thoughts or ideas. Look at the following lists.

TRANSITIONAL WORDS THAT LINK THOUGHTS

again	besides	last
also	further	likewise
and	furthermore	moreover
and then	in addition	next

TRANSITIONAL WORDS THAT COMPARE LIKE IDEAS

also	in the same way	resembling
as well as	likewise	similarly

TRANSITIONAL WORDS THAT CONTRAST IDEAS

after all	granted	on the contrary
although	however	on the other hand
but	in contrast to	otherwise
conversely	in spite of	still
even though	nevertheless	yet

TRANSITIONAL WORDS THAT SHOW SEQUENCE AND TIME

after	earlier	last
afterward	first, second, etc.	later
at the same time	following	next
before	in the first place,	simultaneously
during	etc.	while

TRANSITIONAL WORDS THAT SHOW CAUSE AND EFFECT

accordingly	consequently	since
as a consequence	due to	then
of	hence	therefore
as a result of	it follows that	thus
because		

TRANSITIONAL WORDS THAT EMPHASIZE

certainly	in fact	truly
clearly	surely	undoubtedly
indeed	to be sure	without a doubt

TRANSITIONAL WORDS THAT SUMMARIZE

consequently	in conclusion	thus
finally	in short	to sum up
in brief	in sum	

Because transitional sentences perform such a vital function in a story, they must be clearly and precisely written. A sentence error here can destroy the logical movement of ideas and ruin coherence.

OTHER TRANSITIONAL TECHNIQUES

Constructing a transitional sentence by choosing the appropriate word or phrase from the list is one way to create order and flow within a story. But there are others. Two useful stylistic techniques are *repetition of words or phrases* and *repetition of sentence structure*.

In the following extended, four-paragraph lead, note the repetition of *it/it's* and the repeating sentence patterns:

It looks like silt, smells like Lake Erie on a bad day, tastes like week-old cod and costs almost $3 an ounce. And everybody's buying it.

"It's the most potent food on earth," claims one devotee-turned-distributor.

"It's another gimmick to rip people off," insists a local physician.

It's Spirulina maxima, a spiral-shaped blue-green alga.
—Willamette Valley Observer

In the next example, note how a master of stylistic repetition creates movement and rhythm by repeating phrases and sentence structure. Note also the purposeful use of the run-on sentence. This is Winston Churchill addressing the House of Commons in June 1940:

We shall fight in France, we shall fight on the seas and oceans, we shall fight with growing confidence and growing strength in the air, we shall defend our island, whatever the cost may be, we shall fight on the beaches, we shall fight on the landing grounds, we shall fight in the fields and in the streets, we shall fight in the hills; we shall never surrender.

CHAPTER 4

AGREEMENT—RULES, EXCEPTIONS AND COMMON SENSE

One of the biggest problems in grammar (is/are) maintaining harmony or agreement among sentence elements.

Indeed, agreement is one of those trouble spots that (causes/cause) confusion for writers at all levels.

The preceding sentences illustrate two common *agreement* problems. Writers face these problems daily; however, the issue is more complicated than proper identification of subject, verb, pronoun and antecedent. This chapter examines these five areas of agreement:

- subject–verb
- pronoun reference
- tense agreement
- parallelism
- gender agreement

Like many other areas of grammar, agreement is not always clear and straightforward. *A number* of rules *are* easy to follow; *some are* vexing; but *none is* without logic. We hope this chapter will help you easily solve most of the agreement problems you will face in your writing.

Remember that the rules of grammar are supposed to instill order in your writing. However, when rigid adherence to a rule results in awkward writing, don't abandon the rule; consider rewriting. Unfortunately, some writers resort to the former option, as in this sentence:

Everyone who is a citizen should exercise their right to vote.

The writer considered it awkward to write "*his or her* right to vote" to make the personal pronoun agree in number with the singular subject (everyone). While we don't agree with that judgment, we wonder why the writer opted to violate a basic rule of agreement (*pronouns must agree with their antecedents in number*) when this simple rewrite could have solved the problem:

All citizens should exercise their right to vote.

With that preface, let's *agree* that we'll maintain both rules *and* common sense as we march through this chapter.

SUBJECT-VERB AGREEMENT

You probably can recite this venerable rule in your sleep:

■ **The verb must agree with the intended number of the subject.**

This deceptively simple rule actually calls for two steps: *identifying the real subject* and *determining whether the subject's meaning is singular or plural.* The first step is relatively easy; the second occasionally sends even seasoned writers into fits of frustration.

From your earlier reading you know what a subject *is not:*

□ It is *not* the object of a preposition.

> Among the constitutional <u>rights</u> we cherish <u>is</u> <u>freedom</u>
>   (obj. of   (verb)(subj.)
>   prep.)
> of speech.

(*Freedom* is the real subject. *Rights,* the object of the preposition *among,* is plural, and it is close to the verb; but it has no effect on the verb's number. Because of the alignment of this sentence, it is called *inverted.*)

□ It is *not* the object of a gerund.

> <u>Stimulating</u> investment <u>opportunities</u> <u>has won</u> new friends
> (subj.—ger.)   (obj. of ger.)   (verb)
> on Wall Street for the treasury secretary.

(*Stimulating,* a gerund, is the real subject. *Opportunities,* the gerund's object, cannot influence the verb's number.)

□ It is *not* a phrase that is parenthetical to the real subject.

> The foreign aid <u>appropriation,</u> <u>as well as two anti-</u>
>   (subj.)   (paren.
> <u>nuclear bills,</u> <u>was sent</u> to the subcommittee.
>   phrase)   (verb)

(Phrases such as *along with* and *as well as* merely modify the real subject of a sentence. They do *not* turn that subject into compound, or plural, construction.)

□ It is *not* the expletive *there* or *here.*

> <u>There</u> <u>are</u> fewer housing <u>starts</u> in the country this month.
> (expl.) (verb)   (subj.)

(In these constructions the real subject follows the linking verb.)

To recap this discussion of "false subjects," here is a list of correct subject-verb combinations; both sentence parts are underlined:

> The <u>rate</u> of homicides <u>is</u> climbing.
>   (subj.)   (verb)

<u>Writing</u> country songs <u>is</u> Homer's ambition.
  (subj.)   (verb)

The hardware <u>store</u>, along with the pharmacy, <u>was</u>
             (subj.)   (verb)
demolished.

(*Note:* This sentence may be grammatically correct, but it is not economical journalistic style. A better sentence would be "The hardware store and pharmacy were demolished.")

Here <u>are</u> the <u>subjects</u> the president will discuss.
     (verb)   (subj.)

Now that we have gone through the back door to show what the subject *is not,* let's examine what the subject *is.* You will recall that in the discussion of sentences in Chapter 3, the subject is often the starting point of a sentence. Most often it is a noun or a pronoun, and it generally is a person, place or thing. It generally appears before the verb, although it may follow the verb in certain constructions. It is directly connected to the verb in creating action or in being acted upon.

Identifying the intended number of the sentence's subject often requires more analysis. Let's examine this area in three ways: when the subject is *always singular,* when it is *always plural,* and when it *could be both.*

THE ALWAYS-SINGULAR SUBJECT

This area features several firm rules that should give you little trouble:

- **When used as a subject, the pronouns *each, either, anyone, everyone, much, no one, nothing* and *someone* always take singular verbs.**

   Everyone <u>has</u> been invited to the grand opening.

   Much <u>has</u> been said about the economy, but little has been done about it.

   Each of the wines <u>has</u> its special personality.

The logic of this rule is clear if you think of anyone as "any one person," nothing as "not one thing" and so forth.

- **When *each, either, every* or *neither* is used as an adjective, the noun it modifies always takes a singular verb.**

  Every cask of wine <u>was</u> spoiled.

  Neither option <u>seems</u> very attractive.

- **The personal pronoun *it*, when used as the subject of a sentence, always takes a singular verb.**

  As President Harding said, <u> it </u> <u>wasn't</u> his enemies
                                  (subj.) (verb)
  who brought him down; <u> it </u> <u>was</u> his friends.
                            (subj.) (verb)

- **When *the number* is used as the subject of a sentence, it always takes a singular verb, no matter what the number of the noun in the prepositional phrase.**

  <u>The number</u> of infant crib deaths <u>has risen</u> dramatically
     (subj.)   (verb)
  this year.

Note that the article *the* is more definite than the article *a*. *The number* seems to constitute an organized unit. *A number* refers to an undefined amount; we don't know how many, but we do know it is more than one. Therefore, this sentence would be correct:

  <u>A number</u> of looters <u>were seen</u> running down Harvard
    (subj.)   (verb)
  Avenue.

- **Subjects that stand for definable units of *money, measurement, time, organization, food* and *medical problems* always take singular verbs.**

  Five thousand dollars <u>is</u> the minimum bid for the foreclosed property.

  Twenty-six miles, 385 yards <u>is</u> the traditional distance for the marathon.

  Six hours of waiting <u>has</u> reduced the kidnapper to a bundle of nerves.

  The United Auto Workers <u>is</u> standing firm on its contract demands.

Grits and sausage <u>is</u> a dish I associate with my college room-mate.

Measles <u>wears</u> down parents as well as children.

Plural words that require singular verbs can sound awkward in correct use. For example, if you thought that the first of the preceding sentences sounded strained, you could easily rewrite it to eliminate any conflict:

The county has set $5,000 as the minimum bid for the fore-closed property.

■ **A singular subject, followed by such phrases as** *together with* **and** *as well as,* **always takes a singular verb because the phrase is merely a modification of the subject.**

The tax <u>resolution</u>, together with its amendments, <u>has</u>
   (subj.)   (verb)
been sent to the president for signature.

■ **When all parts of a compound subject are singular and refer to the same person or thing, the verb is always singular.**

The board <u>president</u> and sailboat <u>skipper</u> <u>is</u> Ted Turner.
   (subj.)   (subj.) (verb)

THE ALWAYS-PLURAL SUBJECT

■ **When a compound subject is joined by the conjunction** *and,* **it always takes a plural verb if the subjects refer to different persons or things** *and* **if the subject cannot be considered a unit.**

Two city councilors and one administrative employee <u>were</u> indicted today on charges of grand theft.

(Note that although the part of the compound subject closer to the verb is singular, it still takes a plural verb. The rule is different for *or, neither . . . nor* and *either . . . or* constructions, as you will see in the next part of this section.)

Your stocks and bonds <u>are</u> sure to go up.

- **When they are the subject of the sentence, indefinite pronouns such as *both, few, many* and *several* always take plural verbs.**

  Both <u>are</u> acceptable choices.

  Several <u>have</u> been spotted at the water hole.

- **Well-recognized foreign plurals require plural verbs if they do not denote a unit.**

  The news media <u>are</u> under attack again, a representative of the Society of Professional Journalists charged today.

  (The singular of *media* is *medium*.)

  Her upper vertebrae <u>were</u> crushed in the accident.

  (The singular of *vertebrae* is *vertebra*.)

- **"A number" as the subject takes a plural verb because it does not denote a cohesive unit.**

  A number of ambitious politicians <u>have</u> arrived at the convention.

THE SINGULAR OR PLURAL SUBJECT

Our language contains a series of agreement *exceptions* that seem a bit maddening until they are examined more closely.

- **When a compound subject contains the conjunction *or* or *but* or contains an *either . . . or* or *neither . . . nor* correlative, the *subject closer to the verb* determines the number of the verb.**

  The records or the <u>stereo has</u> to go.
                        (subj.) (verb)

  Neither the lawyer nor his three <u>defendants have</u> in-
                                      (subj.)   (verb)
  dicated a desire to appeal the verdict.

If you must use a correlative conjunction, consider placing a plural subject closer to the verb. Changing the preceding sentence to "Neither the three defendants nor their lawyer *has* . . ." may be correct, but it sounds awkward.

- **Depending on their meaning in each particular sentence, collective nouns and certain words that are plural in form may take a singular or plural verb. Once again, the test of a unit can be applied; if a word indicates that persons or things are working together as an identifiable unit, it takes a singular verb.**

The jury <u>looks</u> concerned.

The audience <u>is</u> stirring; <u>it</u> wants the performance to begin.

Politics <u>is</u> a topic to avoid at parties.

College athletics <u>seems</u> to be a profession today.

Writers often get a clue to subject-verb agreement by determining the meaning of the sentence. When that meaning is decidedly plural, or when nouns imply indefinite amounts, the number of the verb must be plural.

The herd of wildebeests <u>were</u> scattered by the cheetah's attack.

(Many individual wildebeests are scattered; they are not thought of now as a tight group or herd.)

The acoustics in this auditorium <u>are</u> deteriorating.

(The writer is not talking about the sound quality or the concept of acoustics here. The writer is talking about all the *heard sounds* that are bouncing rather badly around this auditorium.)

The mayor's politics <u>are</u> offensive.

(*Practiced political principles* is the meaning here, not the *concept* of politics. If you think of this politician spreading offensive political practices, the meaning becomes more clear.)

If you think a plural verb is required with a collective noun, but it just doesn't look right to you, perhaps consider a minor edit. Instead of

The jury were polled on the split verdict.

(considered individually)

you might write

The jurors were polled on their split verdict.

- **Pronouns such as *any, none* or *some* and nouns such as *all* and *most* take singular verbs if they refer to a unit or**

general quantity. They take plural verbs if they refer to *amount* or *individuals*.

All of the retirement complex <u>was</u> destroyed. (general)

All of the negotiable bonds <u>were</u> missing. (amount)

Most of the day's work <u>was</u> wasted. (general)

Most of the team members <u>were</u> uninjured. (amount)

None of the prosecution witnesses <u>is</u> expected to live to see the trial, according to a police informant.

(In this sense, *none* means *no one witness*.)

None of the stolen goods <u>were</u> recovered. (number)

(The sentence cannot mean that no one good was recovered; it means that no goods were recovered.)

None is a particularly maddening pronoun, and its use causes a great deal of debate. We believe that *none* (*no one*) is almost always singular. However, in the following sentence, a writer's selection of plural predicate nominative (women) makes the intended number of *none* clear:

<u>None</u> of the indicted investment bankers <u>are</u> <u>women</u>.

Still, we challenge you to find more than a handful of examples in which *none* would have to be used in the plural sense for greater clarity.

- **When a subject is a fraction, or when it is a word such as *half, part, plenty* and *rest*, its intended number is suggested by the object of the preposition that follows it.**

<u>Three-fourths</u> of Benton County <u>farmland</u> <u>is</u>
(subj.)   (obj. of   (verb)
                                      prep.)
under water.

<u>Three-fourths</u> of unemployment <u>checks</u> <u>have been</u> delayed
(subj.)   (obj. of   (verb)
                                 prep.)
this month, according to Claims Director Sylvia Smith.

<u>Half</u> of the <u>rent</u>   <u>is</u> missing.
(subj.)   (obj. of (verb)
             prep.)

Half of the rent <u>receipts</u> <u>are</u> missing.
(subj.)   (obj. of (verb)
                prep.)

Occasionally, a *predicate nominative* (see p. 16) may create awkward agreement. Consider this sentence:

<u>Half</u> of the <u>concert</u> <u>(was/were)</u> <u>encores</u>.

Reading our "preposition rule" literally, we must assign a singular verb. However, one could argue that *encores* (a predicate nominative) influences the subject *half* and therefore should have a plural verb. To us, the construction just *sounds* strange. Our advice: Rewrite and give the subject better focus:

<u>Encores</u> <u>were</u> half of the concert.

PRONOUN REFERENCE: LOOKING FOR AGREEABLE ANTECEDENTS

As noun substitutes, pronouns can give a certain economy to sentences. However, pronouns also cause some irritation because of their unfortunate ability to confuse the meaning of a sentence. Because a pronoun must have an antecedent (a noun to which the pronoun refers), its link to the antecedent is important for sentence clarity.

Antecedent confusion abounds in this paragraph:

<u>Engineers</u>, who report to construction <u>superintendents</u>,
(possible antec.)   (possible antec.)
file <u>reports</u> on pipeline completion and <u>summaries</u> of
(possible antec.)   (possible antec.)
safety <u>inspections</u>. <u>It</u> is <u>they</u> who must correct <u>them</u> if
       (possible antec.)(pron.) (pron.)   (pron.)
<u>they</u> have conflicted with <u>their</u> specifications.
(pron.)   (pron.)

A simple way to avoid antecedent confusion is to eliminate the use of the confusing pronoun and use the original reference instead. A revised version of that second sentence might read:

> The **superintendents** must correct the <u>reports</u> that have conflicted with the <u>engineers'</u> specifications.

Without clear connections between pronoun and antecedent, the focus softens. If your readers search in vain for a clear reference for the pronoun, you have engaged in a false economy. It's time to rewrite.

A more difficult problem with pronouns, however, is number and person agreement with their antecedents. Consider these sentences:

> Tobias is one of the worst <u>candidates</u> who <u>have</u> ever campaigned for office.

(Here many candidates are included in the assessment. Tobias is *among* the worst; he does not stand alone. The writer is referring to *candidates* who have campaigned, hence the plural verb. Objects of prepositions can be antecedents; those objects are most often nouns, and a pronoun can substitute for them.)

> Green Fjord is <u>the only brand</u> of sardines that <u>has</u> not given
>   (antec.)
> me heartburn.

(Obviously, there are many brands of sardines. In the opinion of the writer, however, *only one* has not caused heartburn. The relative pronoun *that* substitutes for the singular noun *brand*.)

> The sales manager's <u>presentation</u> was flashy, but not many of the buyers were swayed by <u>it</u>.

(You should not be fooled by the possessive *manager's* here. As a noun substitute, *it* refers to *presentation*.)

> <u>Neither</u> of the men had <u>his</u> sentence reduced.

(As you recall, *neither* takes a singular verb. It follows that a possessive referring to it would stay in the same number.)

A pronoun agrees with its antecedent in both *number* and *person*. Stay consistent, and make your references clear.

TENSE AGREEMENT:
KEEPING TIME IN STEP

It would be grammatical silliness to suggest that you cannot shift tenses of verbs in the same sentence or paragraph. Indeed, you may want to change tenses to show correct historical context:

> Although she <u>was</u> a second-string athlete in high school, Naomi now <u>rides</u> the bench only after she has given her team a comfortable edge.

This is a correct tense sequence. The shift makes sense because it permits us to experience a chronology. Words such as *although* and *after* help us make smooth shifts of tense. But that type of flow does not exist in this sentence:

> Frankie <u>is</u> a dreamer, and no amount of pleading <u>was</u> going to change him.

This is a senseless shift. With no clues except the verbs, the reader loses all time perspective.

In journalistic style, much reporting is done in the past tense. For the sake of immediacy, however, many headlines are written in the present tense. Obviously, the story is more correct historically.

> WASHINGTON—The president <u>said</u> today that he will veto all Senate appropriations that contain new tax provisions.
>
> Headline: President <u>threatens</u> appropriation vetoes

However, journalists often use the "historical present" to create an effect of immediacy or to show that an event, statement or condition is ongoing. The present tense often appears in the lead paragraph, and then the writer shifts into the past tense as the story continues:

> The president <u>says</u> he will not be moved.
>
> At yesterday's press conference in the Rose Garden, he <u>threatened</u> to veto all Senate appropriations containing new tax provisions.

Direct quotes do not work well with the historical present. Even though the tense of the quotation should be preserved, its report should not. This would look odd:

"I will not be moved," the president <u>says</u>.

In this case, it would be better to make consistent use of the past tense:

"I will not be moved," the president <u>said</u>. "I am a fighter, and you will see me fight," he <u>promised</u>.

Another example of the historical present typically occurs in accident stories. This change in tense is correct and logical:

One woman <u>was killed</u> and three others <u>were injured</u> Tuesday night when their sports car <u>skidded</u> on icy roads on U.S. Highway 20 at Santiam Pass and <u>struck</u> a tree.
Dead <u>is</u> Sarah Jane Ridgeway, 28, of Creswell.

Remember that tense agreement is an attempt to preserve historical sequence and context. Look for abrupt and illogical changes of tense. Be consistent.

PARALLEL STRUCTURE

Some problems of tense agreement indicate another writing problem—defects in *parallel structure*. A sentence is parallel when it contains equally weighted items. When a sentence lacks parallelism, its focus softens and its rhythm falters.

COMMON ERRORS IN PARALLELISM

1. *Mixing elements in a phrase or series.*

He enjoys <u>books</u>, <u>movies</u> and <u>driving around</u> in his dune buggy.

Why is this sentence unbalanced? It contains three nouns in a series, but the third noun is a verbal (gerund). It throws off the meter. It reveals a lack of neatness in construction, which could be easily fixed:

> He enjoys <u>reading</u> books, <u>going</u> to movies and <u>riding</u> in his dune buggy.

In the next problem sentence, an adjective clashes with a noun:

> This economic recovery plan is <u>comprehensive</u> and of the utmost <u>necessity</u>.

Using modifiers to complement the linking verb makes it parallel:

> This economic recovery plan is both <u>comprehensive</u> and <u>sorely needed</u>.

2. *Mixing verbals.*

> This is another example of selectively <u>using</u> favorable statistics and then <u>to write</u> a report around that limited sample.

Here a gerund and an infinitive conflict. That portion of the sentence would be parallel if only gerunds were used:

> . . . of selectively <u>using</u> favorable statistics and then <u>writing</u> a report around . . .

Occasionally, you may want to avoid all verbals:

> She is a diplomat who enjoys <u>seeking</u> challenges and <u>to rise</u> to the top of her profession.

Why not use two verbs?

> She is a diplomat who <u>seeks</u> challenges and <u>wants</u> her profession's highest office.

3. *Unnecessarily changing voice.*

Verbs can have *active* or *passive* voices. Writers choose a voice according to the need to have the subject perform the action or to have it acted upon. It is usually preferable to be consistent in voice. Shifting voice generally disrupts the flow of a construction, as in this example:

> The burglars took all the silver and china, but the jewelry and guns were left undisturbed.

It is much simpler to say

> The burglars took all the silver and china but left the jewelry and guns.

(More on voice in Chapter 6.)

4. *Unnecessarily changing subjects.*

> <u>One</u> never should argue with an umpire; <u>people</u> should know that by now.

Besides creating a stilted construction with subjects in two different numbers, the writer also is wasting words. The sentence would read better this way:

> People should know <u>they</u> shouldn't argue with an umpire.

5. *Inappropriately using a clause*
A compound direct object that is broken off by a dependent clause startles and confuses the reader.

> The stock analyst explained the mutual fund <u>market</u>, interest <u>rates</u> and <u>that tax loopholes were becoming difficult to find</u>.

The reader expects to read a short series of objects following the verb *explained*, such as:

> . . . the mutual fund <u>market</u>, interest <u>rates</u> and the <u>scarcity</u> of tax loopholes.

Parallel structure is one of the main building blocks of sentence coherence. Proper use of it does not mean that your writing is rigid. Instead of being too restrictive, parallel structure can give great power and creativity to your work. It can make your writing orderly and easily understood.

GENERIC AGREEMENT

> In construing this notice and whenever the context hereof so requires, the masculine gender includes the feminine and neuter, the singular includes the plural. . . .
> —newspaper legal notice

The growing awareness of sexism in our society and in our language has stirred great debate within the normally restrained circles of grammar. Social and political changes have been the catalyst for challenging some traditional uses of our language. The focus of these challenges has been the treatment of women as an inferior gender in our language. These challenges have forced many thoughtful people to consider how a language can be more equal yet traditional. In a grammatical sense, equal treatment of the sexes is another way to ensure parallelism in your writing.

EXAMPLES OF SEXISM

1. The constant use of the generic *he* when referring to a noun of unknown gender.

> A bank <u>manager</u> is in a position to gauge the financial health of <u>his</u> community.

2. Presumed *maleness* of certain nouns to represent a position or class, even if it appears ludicrous.

> <u>Elizabeth</u> is an outstanding <u>spokesman</u> for her group.

3. *Demeaning* or *unequal treatment* of the sexes.

> The senatorial candidates are <u>successful Wall Street lawyer</u> Harold Smythe and Amanda Johnson, a <u>pert, blue-eyed grandmother</u> of three.

> The <u>men's</u> basketball team posted its fourth straight win last night, but the <u>ladies</u> hung their ponytails in defeat.

4. The use of *courtesy titles* for women (*Miss, Mrs., Ms.*) but not for men.

Few people would concur with demeaning treatment of the sexes or with the presumed maleness of certain words in our language. We believe that the Associated Press Stylebook makes a convincing point in its section on women:

> Women should receive the same treatment as men in all areas of coverage. Physical descriptions, sexist references, demeaning stereotypes and condescending phrases should not be used. . . .

> Copy should not assume maleness when both sexes are involved. . . .
>
> Copy should not express surprise that an attractive woman can be professionally accomplished. . . .
>
> Use the same standards for men and women in deciding whether to include specific mention of personal appearance or marital and family situation.

GENERIC *HE* AND GENERIC *MAN*

The male-dominated status quo of grammar may *seem* to be in the best interest of simple and consistent language use, but it only perpetuates a lie. Rather than make an issue of this, however, we feel it is better to focus on reasonable ways to have gender reference make sense and reflect reality.

Our language is dynamic; it responds to political change and to popular, colloquial usage. Appropriate examples here, with new usage in parentheses, include:

postman (postal carrier)

fireman (firefighter)

spokesman (representative, spokesperson)

councilman (councilor)

anchorman (anchor, reporter)

These "new" words are not awkward. They are truly generic and more representative of reality. When you write, be alert for words and constructions that are not parallel with real life. The last time we checked the statistics, women outnumbered men both in U.S. population and in enrollment in schools of journalism! Therefore, presuming maleness of citizens or students in your writing is clearly inconsistent with reality. Tradition has its place—but not when it puts communication in a false light.

As a further illustration, here is our evaluation of several sentences, all trying (generally) to convey the same thought:

> A writer can succeed if <u>he</u> is willing to market as well as create.
>
> (Clearly sexist construction, it presumes maleness.)

A writer can succeed if <u>they</u> are willing to market as well as create.

(The attempt to eliminate sexism results in a blatant error in agreement.)

A writer can succeed if <u>s/he</u> is willing to market as well as create.

(An awkward, unrhythmic solution.)

A writer can succeed if <u>he or she</u> is willing to market as well as create.

(An improved but somewhat awkward solution.)

Writers can succeed if <u>they</u> are willing to market as well as create.

(An accurate and acceptable solution.)

Our guidelines for achieving proper gender agreement in your writing are brief and realistic:

1. Avoid the presumption of maleness in your writing unless it is accurate in context.

2. Don't demean sexes with stereotypes or unflattering treatment.

3. Avoid courtesy titles such as *Mr.* and *Ms.* Most people have first and last names. On first reference, use a person's entire name; on second and succeeding references, use the last name only. If more than one person shares the last name, use either the first name (or both names) on the second reference. Careful readers of the Associated Press Stylebook will note that we do not concur with its guideline, which states that a courtesy title should be used for women on second reference—unless it is part of a sports story! Such illogical advice is in embarrassing conflict with AP's lofty advice on p. 70 in this chapter.

Two helpful references on this topic are: Miller and Swift, "The Handbook of Nonsexist Writing" (New York: Lippincott and Crowell, 1980), and Dumond, "*Sheit*" (Tacoma: Dumond Publications, 1984).

Writing for mass communications demands clarity and honesty. Achieving grammatical agreement—whether it is the matching of subject and verb number or making the treatment of sexes parallel—will give your writing the ring of order and truth.

CHAPTER 5

CASE

Case is a grammatical term that describes the *form* of pronouns and nouns in a sentence. Pronouns have three forms; nouns change only in their possessive form. Obviously, pronouns can cause the most difficulty in case selection.

Here are examples of typical pronoun use:

She says the new tax form is frustrating.
(nominative)

The IRS told him to hire an accountant.
(objective)

Their tax returns are going to be late this year.
(possessive)

Although only nine pronouns have some change in case, all nouns change in their possessive form. This change only requires the use of an *apostrophe* and an *s*, but the placement is not always simple. This is discussed on pp. 84–86 in this chapter.

Let's examine all three cases and their use.

NOMINATIVE CASE

When you think of the nominative case, think subjective. The *subject* of a verb, the *complement* of a linking verb or an *appositive* (related word, phrase or clause) of either of the preceding is in the *nominative case*.

He dived into the icy waters of the Des Moines River.

(The personal pronoun *he* is the subject of this sentence.)

It was he who signed the deed.

(*He* is the complement of the linking verb *was*.)

We dreamers have to pay taxes, too.

(*We* is an appositive of the subject *dreamers*.)

Obviously, the nominative case can be used more than once in a sentence: It can appear in every clause.

We printers must fight government repression at every turn; it is we who must oppose the Crown's cleverly disguised thievery.

As you recall from Chapter 2, there are nominative forms of personal pronouns and of one interrogative relative pronoun:

PERSONAL PRONOUNS		INTERROGATIVE PRONOUN
Singular	**Plural**	
I	we	who
you	you	
he/she/it	they	

Use of Nominative with
Linking Verbs

Although use of personal pronouns in the nominative case should give you little trouble, you need to be aware that the nominative case is not always used in certain informal linking verb constructions. The rule that a complement following a linking verb should be in the nominative case (for example, "It was I") is not as entrenched as it might be. In fact, these sentences have been acceptable in colloquial speech for years:

It's <u>me</u>.   That's <u>him</u>.

These sentences read (and sound) better in the objective case simply because the pronoun complement of the subject is close to the verb. However, that does not ring true in all similar constructions. The sentence

It was <u>he</u> who signed the deed

may not sound right, but it is grammatically correct. The objective "feeling" of the pronoun that follows *was* loses force because *he* is next to the subject of another clause—*who* signed the deed. In this sentence, both good grammar and close sounding dictate that *he* stay in the nominative case.

Not many of these constructions find their way into journalistic writing. Although we favor the use of informal style in most of these situations, we suggest that you seek a ruling from your publication. We hope that the decision does not fall on the side of inflexible (and awkward) grammar.

Selecting *Who* in Complex
Constructions

Although there are similar pressures to make the *who/whom* choice more liberal, we believe that writers should be very careful in their selections. Most of us have little difficulty recognizing the correct use of *who* when it is the simple subject of a simple clause:

The Vandals, <u>who</u> were 15-0 before their encounter with the Irish, looked flat in South Bend.

But when the subject *who* is separated from its clause, we may tend to use the objective case incorrectly. In this example, the correct pronoun is in parentheses.

The adviser whom (<u>who</u>) the president said had leaked the information was asked to resign.

Whom is not the object of "the president said." The sentence can be analyzed this way:

The adviser . . . was asked to resign
who . . . leaked the information
the president said (parenthetical information)

As you recall from Chapters 3 and 4, it is necessary to match the number of the subject to the proper verb. It is also important to select the right case if your subject is a pronoun:

<u>Who</u> did he say won the race?

(*Who* won the race he did say.)

A pronoun in a prepositional phrase normally is in the objective case because it is generally the object of a preposition. (For *whom* the bell tolls. To *whom* did you wish to speak?) However, a subject can be present in a clause that functions as the object of a preposition. In constructions such as these, a simple preposition is a *linking device,* much like a relative pronoun or conjunction. If the object of that preposition is not a simple word or phrase, do not automatically assume that the object will be in the objective case:

She had been instructed to give the package <u>to whoever</u> wore a purple cardigan.

Although the object of a preposition normally takes the objective case, the presence of an entire clause connected to the preposition changes all the rules. All clauses need a subject, either stated or implied. Hence, we use *whoever* in the preceding sentence. The nominative choice is clearer when the sentence is rewritten for analysis:

> <u>Whoever</u> wore a purple cardigan was to receive the package.
>   (subj.)

Here's another example:

> He discussed the end of the world <u>with whoever</u> would listen.

Note the two clauses:

> <u>He discussed/whoever would listen.</u>
> (subj.)   (subj.)

CASE IN *THAN* CLAUSES

Beware of comparative *than* clauses when selecting case.

> She is taller than I.

Than is frequently a conjunction. As you know, conjunctions connect whole clauses and phrases. Because the second clause in a comparison is sometimes implied, you must mentally complete it to determine proper case:

> She is taller than I (am tall).

In this sentence the nominative *I* is required because it is the subject of the implied clause.
Than can also be a preposition.

> There is no better salesman than <u>him</u>.

In this sentence the comparison ends with *him*. Tacking on "than he is a salesman" doesn't make sense.
Writers must decide whether they want to imply another clause by using *than* as a conjunction or to end the comparison in the same clause by using *than* as a preposition. Meaning and clarity may be at stake. For example, in the classic Western movie

"Shane" starring Alan Ladd, what did Van Heflin mean when he chided Jean Arthur for wanting to leave their homestead, which was being threatened by an evil cattle baron?

> You love this place more than me.

Did he really mean that she loved the place more than she loved Van Heflin? Or did he mean that she loved the homestead more than he loved it? The sense of the scene seems to fit the second interpretation, but the use of the objective case (*me*) communicates the first interpretation. (Of course, there was a suggestion in the movie that Jean Arthur was falling for Alan Ladd, but that's another story.) In any event, be sure to communicate your meaning.

OBJECTIVE CASE

Personal pronouns and the pronoun *who* also change form when used in the objective case:

PERSONAL PRONOUNS		INTERROGATIVE PRONOUN
Singular	**Plural**	
me	us	whom
you	you	
him/her/it	them	

THE PERSONAL PRONOUN IN THE OBJECTIVE CASE

Use personal pronouns in the objective case in the following ways:

1. *As the direct or indirect object of a verb or verbal.*

> The director accompanied <u>her</u> to the premiere.
> (dir. obj.)

> The proud veteran showed <u>him</u> all his <u>medals.</u>
> (indir. obj.)   (dir. obj.)

Discovering <u>Tommy and him</u> in the store proved fatal
           (dir. obj.)
to the owner.

In the last sentence, "Discovering Tommy and him" is a gerund phrase and is the complete subject of the sentence. However, "Tommy and him" is the object of the gerund.

2. *As the object of a preposition.*

Between <u>you</u> and <u>me</u>, this resolution never will pass.

3. *As the appositive of any word in the objective case.*

The comic books were distributed <u>among</u> <u>us boys.</u>
                  (prep.)   (obj. of
                                 prep.)

The security guards escorted <u>us reporters</u> out of
                           (dir. obj.)
the convention hall.

USE OF WHOM

The relative and interrogative pronoun *who* changes its form to *whom* in the objective case. The *who/whom* choice is one of the more confusing ones in grammar, but it is easier to make if you analyze the sentence properly. Let's look at five examples:

1. <u>Whom</u> did the <u>grand jury</u> name in its indictment?
  (dir. obj.)   (subj.)

Keep in mind that a direct object need not follow the the subject. It can appear before the subject, as in the preceding sentence. This grammatical rerouting should not be troublesome if you break down the sentence more conventionally:

The <u>grand jury</u> <u>did name</u> <u>whom</u> in its indictment.
    (subj.)   (verb) (dir. obj.)

2. <u>She</u> <u>is</u> the <u>woman</u>   <u>whom</u> the <u>grand jury</u> <u>named</u>
 (subj.) (verb) (complement) (dir. obj.)   (subj.)   (verb)
in its indictment.

Identifying the two subjects, two verbs and the complement and direct object in this complex sentence helps you select *whom*, not *who*.

She is the woman (indep. clause)
the grand jury named <u>whom</u> in its indictment (dep. clause)

3. To <u>whom</u> did you wish to speak?
  (obj. of
   prep.)

As the object of the preposition *to, whom* is an easy choice because it is part of a simple phrase. In more complicated constructions, of course, this pronoun could be either the subject or the object of the clause introduced by a preposition. (See the earlier discussion under "Nominative Case.")

4. The president is ready to throw his support to <u>whomever</u>
                                                  (dir. obj.)

   the party nominates tonight.

If you read the entire clause as "the party nominates whomever tonight," you can see the role of *whomever* more clearly.

Some writers get confused about the choice of *who/whom* before an infinitive.

5. The firefighters didn't know <u>whom</u> to elect to its bargaining council.

Some grammarians would call *whom* in this example the subject of the infinitive *to elect.* That's real confusion for you—a *subject* in the *objective* case! It seems more logical to see "whom to elect" as the entire direct object of this sentence and *whom* as the simple object of *know.* It is also helpful to know that pronouns in an infinitive phrase almost never take the nominative case.

Are you going <u>to challenge him</u> in a runoff election?

Do you trust <u>him to deliver</u> the contract?

Do you know <u>whom to notify</u> in the event of an accident?

POSSESSIVE CASE

The possessive case does not usually cause the problems that the nominative and objective do.

In this discussion, let's concentrate on three areas: the form and use of pronouns as possessives, nouns as possessives and the misuse of descriptive nouns as possessives.

Form and Use of
Possessive Pronouns

Personal pronouns have these possessive forms: *my, mine, our, ours, your, yours, his, her, hers, its, their* and *theirs*. Note that no apostrophe is needed with the possessive personal pronoun. (However, some indefinite pronouns, such as *anyone, one, everyone, everybody, another* and *someone* do require an apostrophe in the possessive form.)

> Is this <u>my</u> book? (modifies noun)
>
> No, it is <u>mine</u>. (represents noun)
>
> Is this <u>your</u> book? (modifies noun)
>
> No, it is <u>yours</u>. (represents noun)

When a personal pronoun precedes a gerund in a sentence, the possessive case is preferred because it shows possession or ownership by the gerund.

> The board approved <u>his</u> buying the stock after he filed a financial disclosure statement.

In this sentence *his* modifies the gerund *buying*. Because a gerund is a noun, it is proper to use its pronoun in the possessive case.

In many cases the combination of a possessive with a gerund may result in poor style. The following two sentences, for example, would read better with the underlined simple nouns in place of the verbals:

> The press questioned (his refusing/<u>his refusal</u>) to appear before the grand jury.
>
> I can't accept (your regressing/<u>your regression</u>) into procrastination.

The relative pronoun *who* also has a possessive form: *whose*.

> The Farm Security Administration tried to relocate the Depression-era farmer <u>whose land</u> was ravaged by erosion and dust storms.
>
> <u>Whose camera</u> has color film in it?

Note, however, that the interrogative pronoun *who* does not have a possessive form. *Who's* is a contraction—a compression of two words (*who is*). It is a subject and verb, not a possessive. Be careful not to confuse *whose* and *who's*. If you can read "to whom" into a sentence with *whose* in it, your selection is probably correct.

> **Whose** tofu is this? (To whom does this tofu belong?)
>
> **Who's** making the tofu tonight? (Who is making . . .)

Contractions can also be troublesome with personal pronouns. Some of the most common errors occur with misuse of *its/it's, your/you're* and *their/they're*.

> The price of olive oil soared to **its** highest point in history this morning. (possessive)
>
> Do you think **it's** such a good idea? (contraction of *it is*)
>
> After all, this is **your** show. (possessive)
>
> **You're** going to love the next act! (contraction of *you are*)
>
> The bodies of four hikers were found just one mile from **their** well-equipped camp. (possessive)
>
> **They're** here to select a site for an industrial park.
>
> (contraction of *they are*)

You can add the expletive *there* to the *their/they're* confusion.

> The newly installed junta announced **there** would be no elections until spring.
>
> **There's** a moon out tonight.
>
> **Theirs** was a special love.

Read the sentence carefully for meaning to understand whether a possessive, subject-verb contraction or fill-in word like *there* is needed.

Nouns as Possessives

When creating possessives, many writers are confused by the choice between an apostrophe and an apostrophe plus an additional *s*. They fear they don't know all the rules; they feel as if they are navigating through Australia's Great Barrier Reef at night. True, there are a few rules, but they are not difficult.

Here are eight simple rules, consistent with wire service style, for forming possessives of singular and plural nouns.

■ **If a singular noun does not end in *s*, add *'s*.**

the stock <u>market's</u> rally

President <u>Coolidge's</u> humor

Old-line grammar books have ruled that nouns ending in *ce, x* or *z* (and carrying an *s* or *sh* sound) may carry an apostrophe at the end of the word without an *s*. However, both we and many style manuals feel that most of these words can take an *'s*:

<u>Hertz's</u> management policies

<u>science's</u> need for skilled researchers

the <u>box's</u> contents

(Note, however, the exception in the following rule for those possessives that precede a word beginning with *s*.)

■ **If a singular common noun ends in *s*, add *'s*—unless the next word begins with *s*. If the next word begins with *s*, add an apostrophe only. (This includes words with *s* and *sh* sounds.)**

the <u>boss's</u> machine   the <u>boss'</u> stronghold
the <u>witness's</u> testimony   the <u>witness'</u> story
<u>science's</u> needs   for <u>science'</u> sake

■ **If a singular proper noun ends in *s*, add an apostrophe only.**

<u>Yeats'</u> poetry   Tom <u>Robbins'</u> novels   <u>Paris'</u> cuisine

■ **If a noun is plural in form and ends in an *s*, add an apostrophe only, even if the intended meaning of the word is singular (such as *mathematics* and *measles*).**

<u>poems'</u> meanings   <u>witches'</u> executions   <u>measles'</u> misery

<u>mathematics'</u> theorems   Marine <u>Corps'</u> spirit

- **If a plural noun does not end in _s_, add _'s_.**

  women's rights   oxen's yoke   media's successes

- **If there is joint possession, use the corect possessive form for only the possessive closest to the noun.**

  Tracy and Hepburn's romance

  her husband and children's future

  Katherine and Charles' Porsche

- **If there is separate possession of the same noun, use the correct possessive form for each word.**

  Faulkner's and Robbins' novels

  Tanzania's and Paraguay's allies

- **In a compound construction, use the correct possessive form for the word closest to the noun. Avoid possessives with compound plurals.**

  Society of Friends' annual report

  father-in-law's intransigence

  Postal Service's rate hike

  attorney general's opinion

DESCRIPTIVE NOUNS: NO POSSESSION NEEDED

Rather than using an adjective to modify a noun, writers often pair nouns as a descriptive tool. In these instances the possessive form is not needed because the writer does not want to stress ownership.

DESCRIPTIVE NOUNS	POSSESSIVE NOUNS
alumni relations	alumni's response to the fund-raising drive
wine cellar	wine's bouquet
citizens band radio	citizens' advisory committee
police report on racial	
(noun) (adj.)	
harassment	
(noun)	

In the last example, note that there is no satisfactory adjective to replace *police* preceding *report*; however, *racial*, an adjective, is appropriate before *harassment*. *Race harassment* is both awkward and weak. In that same vein *Congress budget appropriations* doesn't flow in the way that *Congressional,* an adjective, would with the paired nouns.

You should never link too many nouns together for descriptive purposes. Some writers may think that this gives their writing more economy, but they are wrong. Poorly glued constructions like "Bruin basketball team booster club" and "union-management negotiation procedure analysis" sabotage sentence clarity. See Chapter 9 for more about this.

Although you may understand the rules of possession, don't overlook exceptions to these rules in the stylebooks of various publications and wire services.

CHAPTER 6

PASSIVE VOICE

When passive voice is used, sentences are robbed of power. Strong verbs are weakened by this construction, and awkwardness is caused. Although there are reasons to use passive voice, it is often employed unintentionally and unnecessarily by novice writers.

When journalists use passive voice, they rob their sentences of power. This construction weakens strong verbs and causes awkwardness. Although passive voice has its place, novice writers often use it unintentionally and unnecessarily.

Read the first paragraph again. Do the sentences sound awkward? Look at the verbs, the "engines" of sentences. Are they powerful words that propel their sentences? In that first paragraph all three sentences are passive voice constructions. In the second paragraph each sentence is rewritten in active voice. Compare the two versions. If you can recognize the awkwardness and the false formality in the first paragraph, if you can see the lifeless verbs, you are on your way to recognizing—and, in general, avoiding—passive construction.

WHAT IS PASSIVE VOICE?

Voice refers to the form of the verb. The subject *acts* when you use the *active voice* verb form. When you use *passive voice*, the person or thing performing the action becomes the object of the sentence. It does not act; it is *acted upon* by the verb.

The legislature vetoed the bill. (active)

The bill was vetoed by the legislature. (passive)

The bill was vetoed. (passive)

In the first sentence the actor (*legislature*) is performing the action (*vetoed*) on the recipient (*bill*). In the second sentence the recipient (*bill*) is having the action (*vetoed*) performed on it by the actor (*legislature*). The second sentence is actually an inversion of the first. Look at it this way:

ACTIVE CONSTRUCTION

who	did what	to whom
actor	performed action	on recipient

PASSIVE CONSTRUCTION

who	had what done to it	by whom
recipient	acted upon	by actor

The third sentence is also in the passive voice. Here the actor—*who* vetoed—is missing. The recipient (*legislation*) is being acted upon (*vetoed*), but we do not know by whom. Although this sentence, like the other passive voice example, is grammatically correct, it does not do the job we expect of a journalistic sentence. It does not tell us *who* is responsible.

Some novice writers mistakenly think the presence of *is, was* or another form of the verb *to be* necessarily signals the passive voice. Although passive voice construction does make use of *to be* forms, not all *to be* forms are passive voice.

He was counting the ballots. (active)

Here the actor (*he*) performs the action (*was counting*). In order for the sentence to be in the passive voice, it would have to be constructed like this:

The ballots were counted by him. (passive)

Note that *ballots*, the recipient of the action, is now the subject of the sentence. The actor, *he*, which was the subject of the first sentence, now appears as the object *him*.

In the following sentence, *was* does signal a passive voice construction:

He was robbed. (passive)

This sentence is passive because *he* is the recipient of the action, not the one performing the action. The actor, the person responsible for the robbery, is missing.

He was robbed by a knife-wielding teenager.

(passive, subject supplied)

A knife-wielding teenager robbed him. (active)

Don't try to identify passive voice by the tense of the verb. Instead, find the verb and ask: who or what is performing this action? If the actor (the *who*) is missing, or if the actor is having the action performed on it rather than directly doing the action, then the sentence is passive.

Let's take another look at two of the sentences in the first paragraph of this chapter:

When passive voice is used, sentences are robbed of power.

(*Who* uses passive voice? *Who* robs sentences?)

When journalists use passive voice, they rob their sentences of power. (active voice)

Strong verbs <u>are weakened</u> by this construction, and awkwardness <u>is caused</u>. (*What* weakens? *What* causes?)

This construction <u>weakens</u> verbs and <u>causes</u> awkwardness. (active)

Now that you can identify passive voice, the next step is deciding if there is a valid reason to use it. Although passive voice does have a purpose, writers often use this construction unintentionally. First consider the problems caused by unnecessary use of passive construction.

DISADVANTAGES OF
PASSIVE VOICE

1. Passive voice saps the verb of its power. In passive voice construction the verb is often preceded by an auxiliary verb (a form of the verb *to be*) and followed by a preposition (usually *by*). These words add clutter and take away the directness of the action being performed. Without a strong, direct verb, a sentence is often listless.

The veto was overridden by the Senate. (passive)

The Senate overrode the veto. (active)

Passive voice construction can also bury the real verb of the sentence. Look what happens to the strong, direct verb *accused* in the following sentences:

The governor <u>accused</u> the press of sensationalism. (active)

<u>Accusations</u> were made by the governor about . . . (passive)

The passive voice sentence changes the verb *accused* into a noun, *accusations*. The result is a lifeless construction.

2. Passive voice can make a sentence unnecessarily awkward by reversing the "who did what to whom" relationship. Subject-verb-object is almost always the clearest, smoothest construc-

tion. It is also the most succinct. Changing the order means adding unnecessary words.

> The car was smashed into by a school bus. (passive, awkward)

> A school bus smashed into (or collided with) the car. (active)

3. Passive voice creates false formality. It can make a sentence sound impersonal and stilted.

> It has been shown by numerous studies that insulating your water heater saves energy. (passive, unnecessarily formal)

> Numerous studies show insulating your water heater saves energy. (active)

or

> If you insulate your water heater, you will save energy, according to numerous studies. (active)

Our tendency to use passive voice to create formality may come from term paper writing and textbook reading. As the favorite construction of politicians and scientists, passive voice is all around us. But as journalists we must strive to write simply, directly and unpretentiously.

4. Passive voice may obscure *who* or *what* is responsible for an action. It can hide the identity of the actor from your audience.

> It was decided that the new chicken pox vaccine was both safe and effective.

Who decided the vaccine was safe and effective? This passive voice construction masks the identity of the decision maker. As journalists we have a responsibility to watch the decision makers and a duty to inform the public. Who or what is responsible for an action may be vital to the story and our audience's understanding of it. Consider these two examples and their implications:

> Researchers working for Bigdrug Company, the manufacturers of a new chicken pox vaccine, decided the vaccine was both safe and effective.

> Independent researchers working for the Food and Drug Administration decided the new chicken pox vaccine is both safe and effective.

Correcting Passive Voice

Unless you have a specific reason to use passive voice (see p. 95), avoid it. This means constructing or rewriting sentences in the active voice. Remember, in the active voice, the actor directly performs the action. This does not mean that all sentences will be alike. You can vary construction by your placement of dependent clauses and phrases.

Correcting a passive voice sentence is simple once you recognize the construction. Here's how:

1. Find the verb in the sentence.

2. Ask yourself *who* or *what* is performing the action. When you do this, you are identifying the actor in the sentence. Keep in mind that some passive voice sentences omit the real actor. You may not be able to find the person or thing responsible for the action in the sentence; you have to add it.

3. Construct the sentence so that the actor performs the action.

Now let's go through the three steps:

Mandatory national service for 18-year-olds was proposed by both conservatives and liberals. (passive)

1. The verb is *was proposed.*

2. *Who* performed the action? *Liberals and conservatives.* That should be the subject.

3. Constructing the sentence so that the actor performs the action, we get:

Both liberals and conservatives proposed mandatory national service for 18-year-olds. (active)

Here is another example:

A plan for downtown revitalization is now being discussed.

(passive)

1. The verb is *is being discussed.*

2. *Who* or *what* is performing this action? The sentence doesn't tell us. Here we have a dangerous passive voice construction that

masks the identity of those responsible for the action. Let's assume that as the journalist covering the downtown revitalization story, you know the city council is discussing the plan. The omitted actor is *the city council.*

3. Making *council* the subject, the sentence becomes:

> The city council is discussing a plan for downtown revitalization. (active)

WHEN PASSIVE VOICE
IS JUSTIFIED

Because passive voice construction reverses the order of a sentence from actor-verb-recipient to recipient-verb-actor, it is a useful device when (1) the recipient is more important than the actor, or (2) the actor is unknown, irrelevant or hard to identify.

1. In certain instances the recipient of the action is more important (more newsworthy) than the performer of the action.

> A priceless Rembrandt painting was stolen from the Metropolitan Museum of Art yesterday by three men posing as museum janitors.

The verb is *stolen. Who* stole? The three men. But clearly, what was stolen—the painting—is more newsworthy than the people performing the action. Passive voice is justified in this instance.

> Mayor Jonathan Sidney was arrested last night and charged with indecent exposure.

The verb is *arrested. Who* arrested? The sentence does not tell us. The actor—the person or person performing the action—is missing from this sentence. But because arrests are almost always made by law enforcement personnel, the actor is far less newsworthy than the recipient of the action—the mayor. Passive voice is allowable in this example as well.

2. Sometimes the *who* or *what* performing the action is un-known or is difficult to identify. When the doer cannot be iden-tified or is irrelevant, you have little choice but to construct a passive voice sentence. In this case, passive voice is appropriate.

The cargo was damaged during the trans-Atlantic voyage.

The verb is *damaged. Who* or *what* damaged it? The doer of this action is unknown. The recipient of the action—what was dam-aged—takes the prominent place in the sentence.

Occasionally, an expert writer may use passive voice as a sty-listic device, purposefully obscuring the doer of the action to create mystery and suspense. Of course, this technique is not appropriate for standard news stories, but it may work in a fea-ture story now and then.

SHIFTING VOICES

Do not shift voices in the middle of a sentence. This shifts the focus of the sentence and confuses your audience. Active voice emphasizes the doer of the action; passive voice emphasizes the recipient of the action.

The president decried the plight of the homeless, but the budget for low-income housing was cut.

The focus of the first part of the sentence is *president*, the actor. The focus of the second part is *budget,* the recipient (of the action of *being cut*). The shift is both confusing and awkward. It adds unnecessary words and robs the second verb, *cut*, of its power. The sentence would be stronger and clearer if both parts were in the active voice.

The president decried the plight of the homeless but cut the budget for low-income housing.

Shifts to the passive are disturbingly common after an imper-sonal *one* or *you*:

> When you use a greenhouse, vegetables can be grown in the
> late winter.

The first part of the sentence is in active voice. The second part shifts the emphasis from the actor (*you*) to the recipient (*vegetables*). Keep both sentence parts in the active voice for clarity:

> When <u>you</u> use a greenhouse, <u>you</u> can grow vegetables in the
> late winter.

A Final Word

Active voice creates sharp, clear and vigorous sentence construction. It saves words and helps the verb maintain its power. Use it unless you have a justifiable reason to use passive voice.

PUNCTUATION

Punctuate: 1. to insert punctuation marks in written or printed matter in order to clarify the meaning;

2. to interrupt from time to time;

3. to emphasize.

—Webster's New World Dictionary

Punctuation: Think of it as a courtesy to your readers, designed to help them understand a story.

—Associated Press Stylebook

Punctuation marks are the finish work of sentence construction. Theodore Bernstein, the New York Times editor who devoted a lifetime to good writing, likened them to "traffic signs and signals placed along the reader's road." In addition to smoothing out your sentence framework, punctuation marks are regulators of meter and emphasis. They say stop, pause, prepare for an aside or incidental remark, read this as a question or exclamation, or get ready for a break in a thought.

Punctuation marks are important tools in your grammar. Like the blades and chisels of the woodworker, these marks have specific uses. If you pick the wrong one or overuse another, you will have a poorly crafted product.

Let's briefly summarize the most commonly used marks of punctuation:

- A *period* ends a sentence.

- A *comma,* however, creates only a pause.

- A *semicolon* slows the reader down; however, it isn't strong enough to stop anyone.

- A *colon* tells us the following: You're about to read a list, be introduced to a fragment or a sentence or be given a quotation to read.

- A *dash*—maligned by purists but used frequently in journalism—creates a more abrupt break than the comma.

- *Quotation marks* are "busy beavers." They are supposed to record speech faithfully, signify book titles and point attention to nicknames, among other things.

- A *hyphen* is well-used in our language. It creates economy by joining modifiers that belong together.

- *Ellipses* warn us that something is missing. . . .

- *Parentheses* (they look like this) are used to add needed information without injuring sentence rhythm.

- You really don't need an explanation of the *question mark,* do you?

- Of course not! For the same reason, we won't explain the *exclamation mark!*

We will not discuss the apostrophe here, because it has been treated in detail in Chapter 5, where possessives and contractions were reviewed.

Although there are styles and fads in punctuation, we writers must adhere to logical, consistent rules. Clarity is at stake. We leave creative punctuation to poets, who, essayist Donald Hall says, are "notoriously innovative." Writer Paul Robinson tells us that punctuation, like other areas of grammar, undergoes many changes.

> A single page of Thomas Carlyle, or any 19th century writer, reminds us, for instance, that a comma between subject and verb—for me the most offensive of all punctuation errors—was once perfectly acceptable.

But journalists are simple folk who thrive on consistency. A set of well-defined rules gives that stability. Of course, these rules assume that you understand sentence construction. If you need a review, consult Chapter 3.

PERIOD

The period signals the end point of a statement. It is the most terminal of all punctuation marks. It makes us stop, not pause. Imagine how difficult it would be to read a sentence with internal periods:

> More than 400 searchers. threatened with a methane explosion. continued to search for survivors. of the mine cave-in.

That rhythm may be fine for a telegram, but readers won't hang on for long.

Lack of the period also harms meter, creating the dreaded "run-on":

> Rescue officials said they could not determine if anyone had been trapped in the cave-in searchers continued to work through the night under the threat of another methane explosion.

Because of the need for meter (flow and rhythm) and the need to stop readers before they move on to another thought, we use the period. The period actually has two main uses in writing.

- **Use the period to end a sentence that is neither interrogative (?) nor exclamatory(!).**

  The three board candidates are unopposed.

  Billy Martin asked the umpire whether he needed a loan to buy a Seeing Eye dog.

Most writers would not neglect to insert a period between two sentences because the run-on of thoughts would be too obvious. However, many writers play a loose game with the comma, using it instead of the period in a long construction that should be two sentences. (We will discuss this comma splice in the next section.)

- **Use the period for certain abbreviations and for decimal points.**

  The U.N. General Assembly voted to send a $17.5 million aid package to Somalia.

Abbreviations are space savers. Periods help signal these shortcuts. However, not all abbreviations require periods. *Acronyms* (abbreviations that are pronounceable words—for example, UNESCO), names of certain organizations and government agencies (NBC, UAW, FBI, CIA), and abbreviations of technical words (mph, rpm) do not require periods.

To learn which abbreviations use periods and which ones don't, consult your publication's stylebook and a dictionary.

COMMA

The comma has a multitude of functions. It is used not only for pause but also for clarity. Ironically, it is clarity that suffers when confusion arises over the comma's placement. Equally important, the comma can be used to excess. This overuse has prompted many editors to avoid dependence on the comma.

To get a proper perspective on the comma, let's examine its proper use and then look at some of its inappropriate uses.

■ **Use commas to separate items in a series.**

> Fire Marshal Tom Jefferson said the factory blaze could have been caused by defective wiring, a chemical reaction in a mixing tank or spontaneous combustion.

> The forecast calls for light showers, some clearing and morning fog.

> The new superintendent enjoys sailing, cooking, stamp collecting and gardening.

When the last item in a series is connected by a coordinating conjunction (*and, or, but, nor, for, yet, so*), the comma can be omitted before that conjunction. This is especially true when the series is short or uncomplicated. However, if the series is longer, the comma should be inserted before the conjunction to eliminate confusion.

> Union officials this morning said they would bargain vigorously for the right to determine pension fund investments, an expanded procedure of grievance settlements, and binding arbitration of all contract matters not settled within 90 days of the start of negotiations.

In addition to the last comma in the series, the use of the preposition *for* before all parts of the series would have made this sentence much clearer.

> . . . for the right to . . . , for an expanded procedure . . . , and for binding arbitration of . . .

■ **Use a comma to separate two independent clauses connected by a coordinating conjunction, as long as these clauses don't contain much internal punctuation.**

Seven men were arrested this morning at a methampheta-
mine "factory" on the east <u>side, and</u> 10 more were taken
into custody six hours later.

Volcanic activity continues on Mount St. <u>Helens, but</u> U.S.
Forest Service officials said they will continue to issue climb-
ing permits on a limited basis.

Remember that an independent clause can stand alone as a
complete sentence. A compound predicate (two or more verbs
that serve the same subject) *does not need a comma* because it is part
of the same clause.

The <u>judge</u> <u>fined</u> the men $250 and <u>ordered</u> them to
  (subj.) (verb)   (verb)
perform 40 hours of community service.

(The sentence has one subject, two verbs, one clause.)

Journalistic style favors dropping the comma if both independent clauses of the sentence are short and if the sentence does not
lose its meter. When in doubt, leave the comma in.

The Assembly approved the bill but the governor vetoed it.

- **Use commas to set off long introductory clauses and
  phrases and some shorter clauses and phrases that would
  be confusing without the comma.**

  When the fire alarm went off for the third time that night, the
  motel clerk finally called the fire department.

  Every day, journalists are asked to make sense of an increas-
  ingly complicated world they themselves find hard to understand.

  To Meryl Streep, Oscar is a familiar name.

You can omit the comma for some short clauses and phrases if
no "run-on" occurs in the sentence—that is, if the meaning of
the introductory segment remains distinct from the rest of the
sentence. A comma is not necessary here:

For six nights flood waters threatened the future of Fort
Wayne.

- **Use commas to set off non-restrictive (non-essential) clauses, phrases and modifiers from the rest of the sentence.**

Let's look first at what is essential to the meaning of a sentence. *Essential* clauses, phrases or words do not need to be set off from the rest of the sentence. There are *restrictive*.

> Two sisters who sought refuge in a church died when the tornado slammed into the building.

(The subordinate clause "who sought . . ." limits the meaning of the sentence. One test to determine this is to read the sentence without the clause in question. If you find yourself trying to "fill in" the meaning of the sentence, that clause is essential.)

> Soybean futures that were sold in the last two weeks have been voided by the Chicago Board of Trade.

(Not all soybean futures have been voided—only a specific group of sales. Because the clause is essential to the meaning of the sentence, no comma is needed. Note that in a restrictive clause the pronoun *that* is used instead of *which*. If the clause is not essential to the meaning of the sentence and just provides added detail, use *which* and set off the clause with commas. See also the entry in Part Two for *that/which/who*.)

> Groucho Marx's brother Chico was an orchestra leader later in his career.

(Groucho had several other brothers—remember Harpo, Zeppo and Gummo? Using a comma in the example would mean that he had only one brother. The absence of the comma here reveals the necessity of the name *Chico* to the meaning of the sentence.)

NON-RESTRICTIVE (NON-ESSENTIAL)

Non-restrictive clauses, phrases and words *do* need commas because they are *non-essential*, or incidental to the sentence. Look at these examples and see how they differ from the restrictive constructions.

> Evans, who was denied parole in his last two visits before the board, appears again tomorrow to argue that 15 years of a 25-year sentence is punishment enough.

(This sentence does not depend on the underlined subordinate clause to complete its meaning. Many other non-essential, amplifying pieces of information could have been added: *who celebrated his 48th birthday today* or *who has consistently maintained his innocence.*)

Chateau Montelena, <u>which is one of the more expensive Northern California wineries</u>, won a gold medal for this year's bottling of Chardonnay.

(The subordinate clause about the cost of wines does not have a necessary connection to the award. It is not essential.)

Sam Bradley, <u>the Sioux City spitballer of Boston Braves fame</u>, died last night at 78.

(The underlined phrase is called an *appositive*, a word or phrase that further defines the word that precedes it. It is not essential.)

My stockbroker, <u>Peabody and Sage</u>, recommends that I invest in Tanzanian cashews.

(The underlined phrase is an appositive.)

■ Use commas to separate descriptive modifiers of equal rank.

When a noun is preceded by a string of adjectives, apply this simple test to determine whether those adjectives need to be separated by commas: If you can use these adjectives interchangeably and can successfully insert the conjunction *and* between them, they are coordinate and require a comma.

Given that test, the modifiers in the following sentence would not need a comma:

Meteorologists forecast another <u>cold Midwestern</u> night.

(You can't read "cold *and* Midwestern night" into it.)

When you add a coordinate modifier, the sentence changes:

Meteorologists forecast another <u>cold, dreary</u> Midwestern night.

(You can read "cold *and* dreary" into this sentence. They modify "Midwestern night" equally.)

These sentences show the proper use of commas:

Scientists will not predict the next activity of the <u>fickle, explosive</u> volcano.

The <u>vacant, mournful</u> eyes of the rescue team revealed the story of the disaster.

- ## Use commas to set off parenthetical expressions.

A parenthetical expression is similar to a theatrical aside. It is not part of the main (onstage) conversation but is intended to give extra information in a quieter tone. These statements could be put in parentheses, but that might be too formal and stilted. Use commas to create shorter pauses without disrupting the flow of the sentence.

These same council members, <u>you may recall</u>, voted themselves a 35 percent pay increase last year.

Because the parenthetical expression lacks directness, you probably will not use it much in straight newswriting. However, it is occasionally well-suited for column and editorial writing.

- ## Use commas when the absence of a pause can cause confusion.

For the mayor, going fishing is enough of a vacation.

Circling the brewery, workers kept a silent vigil to protest unsafe working conditions.

Although it is important not to overuse the comma, it would be a false economy to waive its use in the preceding two examples. The pause is necessary for clarity.

- ## Use commas to set off participial phrases that modify some part of the independent clause.

The Senate adjourned today, <u>having successfully defeated a filibustering attempt</u>. (phrase modifies *Senate*)

Your publication's stylebook specifies many other examples of comma use. Some may be obvious to you.

1,250—but 999 and 2450 Farmount Road.

She is a resident of Toledo, Ohio.

Dead is Tom Jacobsen, 47.

David, will you answer the door?

We know, really we do, that we don't, you know, need a lot of, well, you know, a great many, commas in a sentence. We know that the comma is meant to improve flow, not to obstruct it. The first sentence in this paragraph is a form of literary stammering brought on by poor construction and comma overuse. Writers and editors must be careful to avoid excessive use of the comma.

Here are some rules that can help you avoid comma overuse:

- **Do not use a comma to separate two independent clauses that are not joined by a coordinating conjunction.**

Violating this rule produces the *comma splice,* one of the most common errors in punctuation. It looks like this:

> The inflation rate dipped to 3 percent, the unemployment rate stayed constant.

Using a comma to link two independent clauses (which could stand alone as two sentences) does not help sentence flow and clarity. Break the sentence in two; or you can do two other things:

- Use a semicolon to link the clauses.

> The inflation rate dipped to 3 percent; the unemployment rate stayed constant.

- Use a coordinating conjunction with a comma.

> The inflation rate dipped to 3 percent, but the unemployment rate stayed constant.

- **Do not use a comma to introduce a subordinate clause.**

The use of a comma before the conjunction *because* is one of the biggest offenders. *Because* introduces a dependent clause. It is not a coordinating conjunction; it does not join two clauses of equal rank. *Because* helps explain a statement in the main clause.

> The mayor decided to visit the protest site because she needed a firsthand report.

No comma is needed here because the conjunction is not coordinating equal clauses. That is why *and, but* and *or* often require commas; they are called coordinating conjunctions because they link clauses of equal weight. (See Chapter 2 under "Conjunctions" for a listing of conjunctions that do not coordinate.)

Note that if the subordinate clause is being used to introduce the sentence, a comma is required:

> Because she needed a firsthand report, the mayor decided to visit the protest site.

- **Do not use a comma to separate a noun or pronoun from its reflexive.**

A reflexive is any one of the "self" pronouns *(myself, himself)* used to intensify or accent the noun or pronoun preceding it. A comma is not needed to set off the reflexive:

> Bryant himself will discipline the players.

- **Do not use a comma between a word and a phrase that amplifies it if it will create a "false series."**

This sentence, as punctuated, is bound to cause confusion:

> Rescuers discovered seven bodies, six transients and one firefighter.

Unless the writer meant to say that 14 people were discovered and that seven of them were dead, the comma after *bodies* is wrong. A colon or dash would be more effective in separating the two ideas:

> Rescuers discovered seven bodies—six transients and one firefighter.

- **Do not use a comma to precede a partial quotation.**

> The mayoral candidate charged that the incumbent was "a charlatan of the lowest order."

No comma is needed because the quoted material is the predicate nominative of the verb *was*. Because the quoted material is dependent on the rest of the sentence for its context, that material need not be set off by a comma.

If the quotation is a full sentence, however, it should be preceded by a comma:

> The defense counsel asked, "How would you like to be sent to prison for a crime you didn't commit?"

A good writer uses the comma for clarity and meter. If your sentences contain traffic jams of commas, review those sentences. Perhaps they are too long and too busy. Be brief, be crisp; be sparing in your use of the comma.

Semicolon

The semicolon is a more formal mark of punctuation than the comma. It is half comma, half period. It indicates more than a pause; it is a break but not a stop. It is more inflexible than the comma or period; it carries a grammatical authority that some writers would just as soon avoid in their work. For this reason, perhaps, the semicolon is used infrequently in newswriting.

Journalists often opt for two separate and shorter sentences rather than joining two independent clauses with a semicolon. They may choose to break up a series of thoughts normally punctuated by semicolons in order to avoid long clauses and phrases.

Their hesitance to use the semicolon shows their dependence on the period. They equate the "full stop" with simplicity and clarity. The semicolon apparently doesn't project that image. However, you can see evidence of the semicolon on the editorial pages of your newspaper.

You should be aware of the proper use of the semicolon. It has three main uses:

- **Use semicolons to join independent clauses not connected by a coordinating conjunction.**

> Hayes launched his desperation shot for a three-point play; it
> nudged the backboard and hit the floor as the buzzer
> sounded.

If those two clauses had been connected with the coordinating conjunction *but*, a comma would have sufficed:

> . . . for a three-point play, but it hit . . .

Some writers prefer the use of the coordinating conjunction because it gives more specific direction to the reader. Others would look at these two long clauses and break them into two sentences.

It's important to note that the words *however, moreover, nevertheless* and *therefore* are not coordinating conjunctions. They are *conjunctive adverbs*. They do not coordinate clauses of equal rank. When one of them separates two independent clauses, a semicolon is required.

> "This budget is tentative; however, I would be less than
> honest if I didn't tell you that I urge its immediate adoption,"
> Baker told the board.

As we mentioned earlier in the "Comma Misuse" section, using a comma here to separate the two clauses would cause a *comma splice*.

Semicolons also are needed when more than two independent clauses are linked in a series—even when the last part of the series is connected by a coordinating conjunction.

> Surely the potential casualties are sobering; probably the po-
> litical opposition in Israel would exploit any success short of
> total; and Israel, for all its public defiance of U.N. hypocrisy,
> does not relish the inevitable condemnation.
> —William Safire

■ **Use semicolons to separate internally punctuated independent clauses joined by a coordinating conjunction.**

When you punctuate a clause internally with commas, you can't use a comma to separate that clause from another. A semicolon is needed to create a more abrupt stop:

> The Klansmen, who number more than 50,000, threatened to march through the tense city; but their application for a parade permit was immediately denied.

As you can see, brief, crisp news style often impels you to break up this construction into two sentences.

■ **Use semicolons to set off parts of a series that also contain commas.**

> Killed in the early morning collision were Aaron Jepsen, 37, of Brookings; his wife, Rhona, 32; their children, Tom, 12; Betty, 9; and Richard, 4.

The main function of the semicolon here is organization. It tidies up elements of a series so that they remain distinct.

How often should the journalist use the semicolon? Writer-educator Paul Robinson tells us that semicolons can be used too often "to gloss over an imprecise thought," He adds:

> In exasperation I tried to confine my own use of the semi-colon to demarking sequences that contain internal commas and therefore might otherwise be confusing. . . . But the semicolon has become so hateful to me that I feel almost morally compromised when I use it.
> —The New Republic

We believe the semicolon is helpful when it clarifies boundaries in a series containing commas. But we would urge you to avoid using the semicolon to connect two independent clauses. If you must use it, be sure that the two clauses actually need some connection and that they wouldn't be better off as separate sentences. Don't write:

> The car slid off the roadway into the muddy embankment; the police arrived later to find that no one had survived

when you could write:

> The car slid off the roadway into the muddy embankment. When police arrived later, they found three bodies crushed by the overturned car.

As you can see, merging two strong thoughts into one construction can be economical, but it may not give you the completeness and creativity that two sentences can.

Think of the semicolon as a clarifier, not an economizer.

COLON

The colon presents ideas with a flourish. It announces. It may announce complete sentences, lists, quotations or dialogue.

PROPER USE OF THE COLON

When the colon is used to introduce a complete sentence, the first word of that sentence should be capitalized.

> In the summer of 1968, Johnson conceived a typical triple play: If Chief Justice Warren would retire, Fortas could become chief and an old Texas crony, Homer Thornberry, could be put in Fortas' place.
> —James J. Kilpatrick

When a colon is used to introduce a word, phrase or clause that is not a complete sentence, the first word following the colon should not be capitalized.

> In the movie classic "The Graduate," Dustin Hoffman learned the one word that would guarantee his successful future: plastics.

When the word or phrase following the colon is short or seems to require a more abrupt break, many writers use the dash.

> He thought he had only one choice—suicide.

The selection is purely a matter of preference. The dash is more informal than the colon. Avoid using both the colon and the dash in the same piece of writing.

Here are some other uses of the colon:

- **Use colons to introduce quotations that are longer than one sentence and to end paragraphs that introduce quotations in the next paragraph.**

  The judge eyed the defense attorney and told him in carefully measured words: "Your conduct in my courtroom has defaced justice. I am putting you in jail for 45 days for contempt."

  Here is the text of the president's speech:
  "Good evening, my fellow Americans. . . ."

- **Use colons to show the text of questions and answers.**

This can take two forms:

  Q: And then what did she do?
  A: She put the gun on the table and called the cops.

  Sneed: Senator, I have done my best to contribute to this discussion.
  Ervin: Somebody told me once when I was representing a case; he said, "You put up the best possible case for a guilty client."

As you can see, use of the colon here eliminates the need to use quotation marks unless the dialogue itself quotes other material.

- **Use colons to show times and citations.**

  She ran the 5,000 meters in 15:40:08.
  Psalm 101:5 tells us of the danger of slander.

WHEN NOT TO USE THE COLON

- **You do not need the colon if you are introducing a short list without the words *the following*.**

  The committee decided to interview Long, Henry and Jacobsen.

- **You do not need a colon when introducing a direct quotation of one sentence or less. A comma is sufficient.**

Dash

Some wags claim that journalists invented the dash—that item of punctuation longer than a hyphen, less formal than a colon and more direct than parentheses—to impress readers with information that needed to be abruptly introduced. Actually, the dash has been with us for a long time. In formal grammar its primary uses are to change direction and to create emphasis.

However, journalists may be rightfully accused of using the dash to excess or of using it when a comma, a colon or parentheses might be more skillfully employed. We believe the dash should be used sparingly because it is a startling mark of punctuation. If it is used too often, its impact is lost.

Let's look at the two main uses of the dash in journalistic writing.

- **Use the dash to end a sentence with a surprising or ironic element.**

   The tall, distinguished-looking man entered the country with a valid passport, two pieces of leather luggage, an expensive camera around his neck—and 16 ounces of uncut heroin in the heels of his shoes.

You can see that a comma here would not be as effective in changing meter and warning the reader of a break in thought. Using this reasoning, you would not want a dash in this ordinary sentence:

   House Democrats today approved a change in spending limits for welfare, housing subsidies and insurance.

That series is similar in theme. Adding a dash would give the sentence false drama.

- **Use a dash to set off a long clause or phrase that is in apposition to the main clause when it makes the information clearer and more distinctive.**

   The closing ceremonies of the Olympics—a dazzling spectacle of America through Hollywood sunglasses—started a marathon of self-congratulation at the network.

> Jabbar—long on talent, long on patience and more than ever long in tooth—has a secure claim on "the grand old man of basketball."

A comma usually suffices in a shorter appositive that does not require an abrupt break.

> Baker, the Mudhens' far-ranging outfielder, proved his mettle again today with a rifle throw that eliminated a scoring threat at the plate.

The dash might also be used to set off both parenthetical expressions and a series of items in the middle of a sentence. But we recommend you make these uses rare and concentrate on the two main uses of the dash. The dash is supposed to be an infrequently used piece of punctuation. Make your reader take notice of it.

Quotation Marks

Quotation marks are schizophrenic. They can be a tool of truthfulness when they give a faithful reproduction of what was said. They can also be a weapon that belittles what was said. What impressions do quotation marks create in these sentences?

> "I believe we can correct this situation," the bank manager said.

(This seems to be a straightforward reproduction of what was said.)

> The bank manager said her office could correct the "situation."

(Placement of quotation marks around *situation* makes us suspicious. What is so strange about this situation? If it is something different from a situation, why put it in quotation marks? Why not call it something else?)

You can change the flow and character of a sentence by the way you use quotation marks. Let's look at the appropriate use of this punctuation mark in writing and then list how other marks of punctuation are used with quotations.

■ **Use quotation marks to enclose direct quotations and dialogue.**

"You must remove this offensive book from your library shelves," the irate citizen told the board.

"Will you be there tomorrow?" he asked.
"I'll try," she said curtly.
"I need to see you."
"I'll try."

Avoid the unnecessary use of partial quotations. Sometimes a paraphrase will do. So instead of

Board President Ann Armes said that completion of the third nuclear power plant is necessary if "we are to maintain our high bond rating"

you might write

Completion of the third nuclear power plant is necessary to preserve the board's high bond rating, according to President Ann Armes.

The partial quotation works best if the language or style of what is quoted is distinctive or colorful. It would be difficult to paraphrase this effectively:

Sen. Tony Meeker, R-Amity, compared the higher education system to a dinosaur that's "going to fall in the tarpits and become a fossil."

For the same reason, avoid wrapping quotation marks around single words if it results in an inaccurate representation. We generally put these marks around unfamiliar terms on first reference, around slang words and around words used sarcastically or ironically. But don't overdo it.

A wage freeze is in effect.

His luck ran into a "freeze" at the track.

John Baker's dreams are a $3 million business.

Tom Anderson's "dreams" have ruined those of 35 elderly investors who spent their life savings on his worthless pyramid scheme.

■ **Use quotation marks for titles of books, lectures, movies, operas, plays, poems, songs, speeches, television shows and works of art. Do not use these marks for names of magazines, newspapers, reference books or the Bible.**

"The Powers That Be"

"Supply Side Economics: A Case for Restraint"

"Madame Butterfly"

"The Road Not Taken"

but

The Seattle Times

Mother Jones

Physicians Desk Reference

■ **Use quotation marks for nicknames.**

"Wrong Way" Corrigan

John "The Duke" Wayne

USE OF OTHER PUNCTUATION WITH QUOTATION MARKS

"Does the question mark go inside or outside?" One of the most frequent questions about quotation marks is the placement of other punctuation marks with them. Like so many aspects of our grammar, that depends.

PUNCTUATION THAT GOES INSIDE QUOTATION MARKS

A bit of dogma first:

■ **The period and comma always go inside quotation marks.**

She said, "The union looked to us for a peaceful solution."

"I had to borrow bus money to get here," the unemployed steelworker told the commissioners.

- **Question marks and exclamation marks go inside quotation marks if they are part of the quoted material.**

  The attorney asked, "Did you actually see her with the vial in her hand?"

  "Give me my dignity!" the speaker urged.

PUNCTUATION THAT GOES OUTSIDE
QUOTATION MARKS

- **Question marks and exclamation marks go outside if they are not part of the quoted material.**

  Have you seen "The Brain That Wouldn't Die"?

  No, I haven't read "The Tofu Diet Book"!

HYPHEN

The dash sets words apart; the hyphen brings them together. It is a tiny bridge that links words for compound constructions and modifiers. Unfortunately, the hyphen can be as frustrating as it is useful. If you use it to join words that need to work as a unit and if you use it to avoid confusion, the hyphen will serve you well.

- **Use the hyphen to join compound modifiers that precede a noun unless that modifier is preceded by *very* or an *-ly* adverb.**

Compound modifiers belong together. They are not part of a series of adjectives and adverbs that can separately describe the word they are modifying. The components of a compound modifier actually modify themselves as they describe the noun.

a **good-natured** person

(This is a compound modifier. *Good* doesn't modify *person*. It modifies the other modifier, *natured*. Together they modify *person*. The person is good–natured, not good and natured. Hence, the hyphen.)

a **sluggish, unresponsive** economy

(This is not a compound modifier. The economy is both sluggish and unresponsive. *Sluggish* doesn't modify *unresponsive*. No hyphen is needed.)

If you can insert *and* between the modifiers and make sense of the new construction, you do not have a compound modifier. A "sluggish and unresponsive" economy sounds right, but a "good and natured" person does not. That should be your signal for a hyphen under this rule, unless the beginning of the compound modifier is *very* or an -*ly* adverb. These words are a clear signal to the reader that a compound modifier is coming. No hyphen is needed in these cases.

very refined person

heavily spiced recipe

but

well-read student

Most compound modifiers are also hyphenated when they follow a form of the linking verb *be*. In that sense, they continue to modify the subject.

The student was well-read.

Make a distinction between a compound modifier and the same set of words that really don't modify anything. It will prevent the improper use of the hyphen.

The last-minute election returns put him over the top.

(*Last-minute* modifies *election*.)

He filed for election in the last minute of registration.

(*Last minute* is the object of the preposition *in*. There is no modification and therefore no hyphen.)

Be sure to identify all parts of a compound modifier. It's not a 30 *mile-per-hour* speed limit. It's a *30-mile-per-hour* speed limit.

■ **Use the hyphen for certain prefix and suffix words.**

To be sure on this one, always consult a dictionary. There are so many exceptions that you will never guess right all the time.
The Associated Press stresses this rule:

■ **Hyphenate between the prefix and the following word if the prefix ends in a vowel and the next word begins with the same vowel (for example, *extra-attentive;* exceptions are *cooperate* and *coordinate*), and hyphenate between the prefix and the following word if that word is capitalized (such as *super-Republican*).**

Prefixes that generally take a hyphen include *all-, anti-, ex-, non-* and *pro-*. If you check a dictionary and stylebook, however, you will find plenty of exceptions.

■ **Use the hyphen for combinations when the preposition is omitted.**

Cheyenne-Omaha train

A 149-122 score

autumn-spring cycle

Ellipsis

We use the ellipsis mark (. . .) to alert the reader that *something has been removed from quoted material,* that the *speaker has hesitated or faltered* or that *there is more material than is cited.*

"We must fight this move . . . ; we must save this plant."

(The original statement was, "We must fight this move by a management that is bent on saving money with no regard for this town; we must save this plant." In the interest of economy and impact, the writer condensed this statement but preserved its accuracy.)

Facing the hostile audience, Baker tried to frame his thoughts. "Under these circumstances," he said, "I feel I can no longer serve this community as superintendent. I have tried my best . . . I have always wanted. . . ." Unable to continue, he left the crowded meeting.

(Note that at the end of a hesitation or at the end of a condensed statement, another period is placed after the ellipsis.)

There are many excellent non-contact sports (squash, racquetball, swimming . . .) that are good for your cardiovascular system.

Remember these rules about punctuation with the ellipsis:

- **Another period comes at the end of the ellipsis, if it is the end of the statement.**

  "This is a difficult time for all of us. . . ."

- **Other punctuation marks, if needed, come *after* the quoted material but *before* the ellipsis.**

  "How would you feel? . . ."

  "We can't stand for this! . . ."

PARENTHESES

The characteristics of journalistic writing—brevity, crispness and clarity—imply that parentheses are not welcome. However, there are times when parentheses can be used effectively. Two of the most common are (1) to signify the addition of needed information and (2) to mark an aside, or something incidental, to the main thought.

Caveat emptor ("let the buyer beware") is a war cry for consumer activists.

He arrived at the bank, only to find it was closed. (It closed every day at noon.)

If you find that parenthetical material is getting too long or too complicated, perhaps a rewrite is in order.

■ **If the material inside the parentheses is not a complete sentence, put the period outside the parentheses.**

He likes decaffeinated coffee (the cold-water extract type).

■ **If the parenthetical material is a complete sentence, but it depends on the sentence around it for context, put the period outside.**

He wrote caveat emptor ("let the buyer beware").

■ **If the parenthetical material is a complete sentence and can stand alone, put the period inside the parentheses.**

Roads were clear this morning despite the heavy snowfall last night. (Reports coming in to the paper said that the Department of Transportation had authorized overtime for three full crews.)

QUESTION MARK AND
EXCLAMATION MARK

■ **If you want to ask a *direct question*, you must use the question mark.**

What's next for Omark Industries?

■ **If your question is *indirect*, no question mark is needed.**

The president wants to know what is happening in Central America.

The exclamation mark should be used only to express a strong emotion or surprise. In journalistic writing you probably will employ it only in direct quotation because of the exclamation's highly editorial nature. You would not write a lead paragraph such as:

James Smith, 26, has been arrested for the slaying of his estranged wife!

Both the exclamation mark and the question mark should be included inside quotation marks if the exclamation or question is part of the quoted material.

In direct quotations, remember that the comma is not necessary if the exclamation mark or the question mark is part of the quoted material that precedes attribution.

"You can't make me testify!" the angry defendant screamed.

"Is this really the kind of economy we want?" the candidate asked the Grange audience.

Punctuation gives order and direction to your writing. It provides clarity, flow, emphasis—even drama. Use punctuation marks wisely and naturally to put finishing touches to your writing.

CHAPTER 8

SPELLING

Scholars tell us that the purpose of spelling is to remove chaos from our language, to bring precision and order to words influenced by a host of pronunciations and linguistic origins. That seems reasonable. Why, then, does this drive toward precision cause us so much anxiety?

"You can't teach someone to spell—it's in the genes," argues one person.

"There are just too many rules and exceptions," laments another.

"I'm not stupid; I'm a good writer but a bad speller," rationalizes a third.

Well, we have good news and bad news for you. The good news is that we agree that learning to spell can be both difficult and frustrating. The bad news is: You don't have any choice! You must learn to spell effectively or at least create an effective system for detecting and correcting spelling errors. If you don't, you're going to be in *s-e-r-i-o-u-s* trouble in the world of mass communications.

Spelling, which creates the same sense of order as does grammar, maintains an honored role in our language. Without consistency in spelling, messages are garbled. The lack of order and uniformity can create real obstacles to communication.

It was the need for uniformity, coupled with a strong spirit of independence, that led to spelling reform in early America, as 18th- and 19th-century lexicographers struggled to remove "British" spellings. Led by Noah Webster, who grudgingly agreed with Ben Franklin that spelling reorganization was necessary, spelling in America took on its own character. *Defence* became *defense, honour* became *honor*, and *theatre* became *theater*. This reform also streamlined such awkward constructions as *publick, darke* and *masque*. Indeed, creating an American dictionary was a revolutionary act.

Today, our information society produces many aids to spelling. For the *logophile* (look it up!), multivolume dictionaries provide as many as 150,000 entries, with definitions, derivations, pronunciation guides and, of course, spellings. For writers linked to the electronic word processor, spelling-checker software monitors as many as 75,000 words. And bookstores abound with self-help guides on learning to spell. We haven't yet heard of hypnotherapy for people with spelling blocks, but stand by.

Of the aids mentioned, we prefer the dictionary because it provides the most depth and dimension. People who check spelling in a dictionary also learn about proper pronunciation and meaning. It is precisely the companion a professional communicator needs.

The active and curious reader always has an advantage in vocabulary and spelling. Reading is the most effective long-term method for improving spelling and word use.

In this chapter, we suggest a regimen of spelling training that we hope will interest and stimulate you. It involves an examination of three areas: *sound, sense* and *structure*, with a look at frustrating exceptions to rules and at troublesome spellings. We believe this basic approach is not overwhelming; we hope it will guide you to more consistent, correct spelling.

Sound

"Sounding" a word by breaking it into phonetic patterns and into syllables can be an effective method of determining the spelling of a word. You will be amazed at how many words you can "sound out" without the aid of a dictionary—and come up with the right spellings. However, this step generally requires the use of a dictionary, which provides a pronunciation guide for each word. Learning the *proper* sound gives you clues about words that have similar spellings but different pronunciations. Look at this trio:

through	cough	bough
(throo)	(kôf)	(bou)

Through this examination, we find that *-ough* has several sounds—but only one spelling.

Looking up words also will show you how many syllables each word contains and which syllable is accented. This gives a finer tuning of the "sound" of a word. Consider, for example, these two nouns:

desert (barren wilderness)

dessert (ice cream)

Their pronunciations differ:

desert is <u>dez</u>-urt

dessert is di-<u>zurt</u> (The accented syllable is underlined.)

This guide won't help you with the *verb* desert (to abandon); it is pronounced like *dessert*. But at least you've covered one distinction.

Examining syllables also will give you a keener ear about proper pronunciation. Here are two difficult spellings, broken into their syllables:

di-lem-ma   sep-a-rate

Checking syllables and sounding them out tell you that *dilemma* has only one *l* and two *m*'s, and that *separate* has an *a* (not "urh") that separates *sep* and *rate*.

Checking pronunciation also makes you aware of silent letters that can fool your spelling. For example, the musical *chord* has a silent *h*, which makes its sound similar to the material *cord*. The mistakenly omitted *n* in *environment* leads to incorrect pronunciation (enviro-ment) and, of course, incorrect spelling. The root word is *environ* (with an audible *n*), meaning "to surround." The same mistake is often made with gover*n*ment and su*r*prise. Taking care with correct pronunciation and being aware of mistakenly silent letters can help prevent many spelling errors.

Have you noticed the spellings of pro*nounce* and pro*nunc*iation in this chapter? These words obviously have different pronunciations.

Homonyms, words that have similar pronunciations but different meanings and spellings, can cause confusion for the careful speller. It is here where *sense* plays an important role.

SENSE

What does this word mean? What is its proper use in this sentence? These two questions are good reasons to reach for a dictionary (something you can't do yet with word-processing software). An added dividend from this search is that you *see* the correct spelling of a word.

Using the dictionary is very helpful for homonyms—similar-sounding word pairs that have different spellings. Here are a few examples:

accept	crews	oar	seam
except	cruise	ore	seem
aisle	discreet	pray	their
isle	discrete	prey	there
bear	grate	principal	they're
bare	great	principle	vain
berry	heard	profit	vane
bury	herd	prophet	vein
cede	hour	rack	ware
seed	our	wrack	wear
complement	lead	rye	where
compliment	led	wry	weather
			whether

Obviously, understanding the sense of a word helps us both in using it correctly and in spelling it right. When we understand, for example, that station*e*ry is writing material and that one writes best from a station*a*ry position, we're not likely to use the wrong spelling.

Consider *interment* and *internment*. Sometimes, sloppy pronunciation makes these two words seem similar. However, their intended meanings in the sentence should be clear. Burying someone is an *interment*; detaining a person is an *internment*. This distinction is cheerfully brought to you by your dictionary.

The contraction *it's* and the possessive pronoun *its* are other examples in which spelling depends on knowing the sense of words. In this case, good grammar requires us to know the difference between *it's* and *its*, but a knowledge of their meanings is a giant step toward avoiding errors in their selection.

STRUCTURE

Just as our language has rules dealing with agreement, case and punctuation, so too does it have rules that control the spelling of many of its words.

Although it may seem that spelling rules are riddled with exceptions, most words are covered by these guidelines. Let's examine several of the key rules—and deal gingerly with the exceptions.

SURVIVING SUFFIXES

A suffix is a group of letters added to a root word to give it new or added meaning. For example, when you add *-ible* to *access,* you have *accessible,* which means "an easy approach." Sometimes, however, suffixes are tacked onto incomplete roots. Take *dispense:* If you want a suffix after it to denote "an ability to dispense," you would add *-able,* and because the last letter of the root is a vowel, you drop it and make dispensable. (As you might expect, the dropping of the vowel doesn't always occur.)

Why, you might ask, do we have *-ible* and *-able* when they mean the same thing? The answer has to do with the history of our language; *-ible* connects with Old Latin–based verbs, and *-able* has Old French and Anglo–Saxon lineage. The use of *-able* or *-ible* gives you a clue to the word's origin. However, you will find that *-able* words outnumber the *-ible* ones.

The other suffixes you should master are *ance/ant* and *ence/ent*. These, too, come from French and Latin, and the *-a* or *-e* choice has to do only with the original form of the Latin and French word. Both *-ance* and *-ence* create nouns from verbs, indicating a state or quality, as in resist*ance* and persist*ence*. Both *-ant* and *-ent* are used to form adjectives, as in resist*ant* and persist*ent*.

With this introduction, we can offer some general rules about the uses of these suffixes:

■ **Not only is *-able* more common than *-ible*, but it also is used mostly with *complete* root words.**

Therefore, we have *work*able, *depend*able and *perish*able *Exceptions:* A few root words drop their final *e* when adding *-able*. These include *desir*able, *excus*able, *indispens*able and *us*able. Fortunately, there aren't many of these! There are many more examples of the retention of the final *e*, such as chang*e*able and notic*e*able.

■ **Only *-able* follows *g, i* and the hard *c* ("k" sound).**

This explains the spelling of navig*a*ble, am*i*able and irrevo*c*able. This is a dependable rule.

■ **The suffix *-ible* is commonly used after double consonants (like *ll*), *s, st,* some *d* sounds and the soft *c* ("s" sound).**

This explains infa*ll*ible and ho*rr*ible; divi*s*ible and plau*s*ible; e*d*ible and cre*d*ible; and for*c*ible and invin*c*ible.

Here are some guidelines to help you distinguish between *-ance* and *-ence* words:

□ *Their sounds.* For example, attend*ance* has an "ah" sound in its suffix, whereas independ*ence* has an "eh" sound;

□ *Your memory.* Here are some of the more difficult ones to remember:

A	E
attendance	existence
descendant	independence
maintenance	persistent
relevant	recurrent
resistant	superintendent

Remember—you have only two choices with these words. When in doubt, look it up. It won't take that long.

EI-IE-OH!

The *ei/ie* dilemma is not overwhelming. These guidelines should help:

■ **The -*ie* spelling is more common than -*ei*. And *i* usually precedes *e* unless it follows a *c* that carries an "s" sound.**

Here are some examples:

BEFORE OR WITHOUT *C*	AFTER *C*
fierce	deceit
hygiene	perceive
niece	receipt
wield	receive

Note: French -*ier* words like *financier* don't violate the -*ei* after *c* rule. The -*ier* just happens to be a standard ending.

It's more demanding to remember these -*ei* constructions:

☐ words with long "a" sounds, such as w*ei*gh and fr*ei*ght;

☐ words with long "ain" sounds, such as f*ei*gn and r*ei*gn; and

☐ five exceptions that just demand memorization: caff*ei*ne, l*ei*sure, prot*ei*n, s*ei*ze, w*ei*rd.

■ **If a *c* carries a "sh" sound, it probably will be followed by *ie*.**

Examples include:

ancient   deficient   sufficient

TO DOUBLE OR NOT TO DOUBLE THE CONSONANT

When you add *-ing* or *-ed* to a word, you generally double a final consonant only if:

□ the word ends in a single consonant. So, *commit* becomes commit*ting* and commit*ted.*

□ that consonant is preceded by a single vowel. Comm*i*t is safe here, so the final consonant can be doubled.

□ the accent is placed on the last syllable. The pronunciation is com*mit* (accented syllable in italic), so our rule is valid. Note these other examples, where all three guidelines are met:

acqui*tt*ed   equi*pp*ing   occu*rr*ing   omi*tt*ed

Understanding this rule, you can see that certain words *will not double* their final consonant. This occurs when:

□ the accent is *not* on the final syllable of the root word. This explains cance*l*ed and trave*l*ing. Note their accents:

cancel   travel

This also explains the spelling of *kid*naped and *prof*ited.

□ no vowel precedes the final consonant. This explains inve*st*-ing; a consonant precedes the final one.

Take note of one other guideline: The suffix *-ment* doesn't require doubling the final consonant of the root word. Because *-ment* begins with a consonant, there is no need to alter the root. So, we have equi*pp*ing but equip*ment*, allo*tt*ing but allo*t*ment, commi*tt*ed but commi*t*ment.

Words almost fail when we discuss the next list of words. They *are* frustrating but not overwhelming. Although reliable rules seem to have been abandoned, sound can be a great help. Examining differences in pronunciations and meanings can help, too.

This list of troublesome word pairs and groups is not comprehensive, but it should help you in many cases.

accumulate	inoculate	religious
accommodate	innovative	sacrilegious
battalion	millionaire	theater
medallion	questionnaire	massacre
census	proceed	vilify
consensus	precede	villain
embarrass	supersede	
harass	recommend	
	occasional	

Some Final Words

Here is a list of difficult spellings that vex many writers—some of the words most commonly misspelled by students and professionals. Notice that many of the guidelines and suggestions mentioned in this chapter can help you spell these words correctly.

Remember: *When in doubt, look it up.* Your credibility as a journalist is at stake.

acceptable	acquit	business	comparable
accessible	adviser	caffeine	condemn
accidentally	argument	calendar	conscious
accommodate	athletic	canceled	consensus
accumulate	bankruptcy	cemetery	courageous
acknowledg-ment	believe	changeable	criticize
	broccoli	commitment	definite

desirable	inoculate	parallel	sheriff
desperate	irascible	permissible	sovereign
deterrent	irresistible	persistent	succeed
dilemma	judgment	potatoes	supersede
ecstasy	legitimate	precede	surprise
eighth	leisure	predecessor	tariff
embarrass	likable	privilege	temperament
excusable	likelihood	procedure	vacillate
exhilarate	loneliness	protein	vacuum
existence	manageable	questionnaire	vilify
financier	millionaire	recommend	villain
forcible	niece	relevant	weird
harassment	noticeable	resistant	wield
hemorrhage	occasion	rhythm	withhold
hygiene	occurrence	seizure	woolly
indispensable	omitted	separate	yield
innocuous			

CHAPTER 9

CLARITY, CONCISENESS, COHERENCE

Every time you choose a word, create a phrase, craft a clause or commit a sentence to paper, you should ask yourself: "What am I trying to say?" Good writing says what you intend it to say: No reader has to backtrack through your story to puzzle out its meaning; no listener has to furrow a brow in confusion.

Good writing begins with clear thinking: You study the information you have and reason through what you are trying to say. Then you make a series of choices, as you ask yourself how best to express these ideas. If you choose carefully and correctly, your writing communicates information precisely, succinctly and logically.

Good writing is no accident.

You, the writer, control both language and ideas. You make conscious decisions every step of the way. In fact, good writing is an unending parade of decisions. On the surface, these decisions appear to be mechanical: spelling, vocabulary, grammar and punctuation. But clarity, conciseness and coherence underlie each choice. As William Zinsser says in his excellent book "On Writing Well": "The game is won or lost on hundreds of small details." Let's begin with that first "detail," that first choice—the word.

Choosing Words

Verbs

We've continually stressed the power of verbs. The verb, we've said, is the engine of the sentence. Without a strong, convincing verb, a sentence can be motionless, lifeless. Using the *correct* verb form is a matter of grammar; choosing the *right* verb is a matter of conciseness and clarity.

Modifying a Verb When You Should Be Searching for a Better One

Our language has thousands of strong, concrete, precise verbs. Learn to use them rather than saddling an imprecise verb with a load of modifiers. If you must tack on an adverb or a series of adverbs to clarify the meaning of the verb you have chosen, reconsider your original choice.

Let's look at a workhorse verb: *walk*. It means "to advance on foot, to move by steps." It describes an action, but the description is far from precise. You may find yourself tacking on adverbs to clarify and further define the verb. The challenge is to express the action clearly and precisely, using the fewest words possible.

INSTEAD OF	USE
walk gracefully	glide
walk drunkenly	lurch
walk purposefully	stride
walk aimlessly	wander

Consider this assortment of verbs, each of which defines and captures a precise meaning of the verb *walk:*

slog, trudge, plod, shuffle, ramble, amble, saunter, stagger, wobble, slink, tramp, march, troop, roam, rove, meander

Adverbs certainly have their place in clear, concise writing, but they are not meant to compensate for inexact verb choices.

Avoiding *Up*

She was chosen to head up the committee.

The mayor has to face up to the problem.

The accident slowed up (down) traffic.

None of these verbs needs the preposition *up*. *Up* doesn't add meaning to these verbs; it takes away their crispness.

She was chosen to head the committee.

The mayor has to face the problem.

The accident slowed traffic.

Beware of *free up* (*free*), *walk up* (*walk*), *wake up* (*awake*), *stand up* (*stand*) and *shake up* (*shake*). In these instances, *up* is more than unnecessary; it's sloppy.

Of course, some verbs need *up* to complete their meaning. *Make* does not mean the same thing as *make up*. *Break* is not synonymous with *break up*. *Up* is necessary for the meaning of *pick up*. In these cases, *up* is not clutter, but neither is it precise, strong writing.

He accused the senator of making up the statistics. (weak)
He accused the senator of fabricating the statistics. (stronger)

The investigation broke up the crime syndicate. (weak)
The investigation shattered the crime syndicate. (stronger)

The economy is picking up. (weak)
The economy is recovering. (stronger)

> The committee will <u>prioritize</u> its concerns, <u>definitize</u> its plan
> and <u>respectabilize</u> its existence. It hopes to <u>concretize</u> the
> plan without <u>fractionalizing</u> the community.

The suffix *-ize* is running rampant in our language. Some people think you can tack *-ize* onto the end of any noun and create a verb. Many of these makeshift verbs are unnecessary. *Fractionalize,* for example, means nothing more than *split.* Other words with longer linguistic histories, like *utilize* and *signalize,* serve no distinct purpose. *Utilize* has come to mean nothing more than *use. Signalize* means *signal.* Not only are many of these *-ize* verbs useless, but they are also grating to the ear, awkward and stuffy. They are not the stuff of clear, concise writing.

Of course, yesterday's awkward jargon is today's respectable word. *Pasteurize* must have raised the hackles of 19th-century grammarians, but not even Edwin Newman, the television newscaster who writes wittily on the erosion of the English language, would be upset about it today. It is difficult to say how many of the newly created, tongue-twisting *-ize* verbs will become accepted additions to our language. While we are awaiting the verdict, we can subject an awkward-sounding *-ize* verb to three tests:

1. Is it listed in the dictionary as an *acceptable* (not informal, colloquial or slang) word?

2. Does it have a unique meaning?

3. Does it have a sound that is, at the very least, not displeasing?

If the word passes these three tests, use it. If it fails, find a different word. Do not *jargonize* and *awkwardize* the language. It may be all right to *pasteurize* milk, but it is not yet acceptable to *zucchinize* a casserole.

INTENSIFIERS

Our spoken language is sprinkled with words like *very, really, truly, so, completely, totally, positively* and *perfectly.* Sometimes we use these words in an attempt to *intensify* an adjective: *really hungry, very tired.* But often they serve no purpose. Perhaps because we have grown accustomed to using these intensifiers when we speak, we find them cluttering our written work as well. Let's consider three problem areas.

INTENSIFYING WHEN YOU SHOULD BE SEARCHING

Using intensifiers to bolster a weak or less than precise adjective contributes to wordiness and lack of precision in writing. Because they are overused, intensifiers often don't do the job you would like them to. They merely take up space. When you find yourself tacking on an intensifier to heighten the meaning of an adjective, look for a different adjective—one strong word rather than two weak words. For example:

INSTEAD OF	USE
very rushed	harried
really fancy	elegant
truly sorry	remorseful
extremely active	frenetic
totally afraid	terrified

Using intensifiers to bolster an adverb can add even more clutter. The intensifier modifies the adverb; the adverb modifies the verb. Now you have three words instead of one. For example:

run very quickly	speed, race
examine really closely	probe, delve, scrutinize
speak extremely quietly	whisper, murmur, mutter

A thesaurus or synonym finder may help you in your search for the one precise word. But the best way to build and continue to enrich your vocabulary is to read.

OVERINTENSIFYING

Sometimes writers don't leave well enough alone. Not trusting the power of words, they write that the marathon runner is "very exhausted"; the worker who has lost her job is "very despondent"; the parents of healthy quintuplets are "totally elated."

When you intensify an already intense word, be it adjective or verb, you do more than add clutter—you sap the word of its strength. Once you have chosen a powerful word, trust it to stand on its own.

CREATING REDUNDANCIES

Redundancy is saying the same thing twice. Later in this chapter, you will read about the spate of redundant expressions that are an unfortunate part of the journalist's vocabulary. Here we want to note redundancies caused by the gratuitous use of intensifiers.

If a building is destroyed by fire, it is destroyed in its entirety. *Destroyed* means "ruined completely; spoiled so that restoration is impossible." Yet journalists write: "The building was completely destroyed by fire." *Completely* is unnecessary. *Completely destroyed* is redundant. The orphan is not *totally deserted*. The concert hall is not *completely empty*. *Deserted* means "forsaken." Either one is forsaken or one is not. If one is, it is "total." A room is either empty or not empty. *Completely* adds nothing. A *correct* answer is, by definition, "perfectly" correct. *Perfectly correct* is redundant.

Know the meanings of the words you use. Redundancies show both ignorance of and lack of respect for the language. Keep wise counsel with your dictionary.

THAT

That performs several grammatical functions. It is an adjective:

That book is a best seller.

(*That* describes *book*.)

It is a demonstrative pronoun:

That is not the issue facing the court.

(*That* takes the place of a noun.)

It is a relative pronoun:

This is a design that will make millions.

(*That* introduces a relative clause.)

It is a conjunction:

> The official admitted <u>that</u> he lied.
>
> (*That* links two independent clauses.)

The most troublesome uses of *that* are as a conjunction and as a relative pronoun. Quite simply, writers overuse it. *That* is often unnecessary in a sentence. If the word does not add meaning, get rid of it. Consider these sentences, all of which would be crisper without *that:*

> The official admitted ~~that~~ he lied.
>
> Government sources say ~~that~~ the report will be released tomorrow.
>
> The dress ~~that~~ Nancy Reagan wore is now in the Smithsonian.
>
> The statement ~~that~~ he made infuriated the committee.

Often all you need do is edit out the useless *that*. However, some sentences demand revision.

> Police recovered the painting <u>that was stolen.</u> (wordy)
> Police recovered the <u>stolen</u> painting. (improved)
>
> The photograph <u>that he took</u> won first prize. (wordy)
> <u>His</u> photograph won first prize. (improved)

That is sometimes used legitimately to link sentence parts. To discover whether *that* is necessary to a sentence, ask yourself two questions:

1. Can *that* be omitted with no change in the meaning of the sentence?
2. Can the clause introduced by *that* be expressed more concisely?

If you answer *yes* to either question, edit or restructure.

REDUNDANCY AND WORDINESS

Ignorance of the real meanings of words, attempts at false erudition, repetition of other people's jargon and sheer sloppiness all result in the journalist's falling prey to redundancies. They not only stand in the way of clear, concise, coherent writing but also are an embarrassment. Here are a few culled from daily newspapers:

mutual cooperation

(*Cooperation* means "acting for mutual benefit." *Mutual* is redundant.)

consensus of opinion

(*Consensus* means "collective opinion.")

remand back to the lower court

(*Remand* means "order back." Also beware of *refer back, repeat again.*)

negotiated collective bargaining agreement

(A collective bargaining agreement is, by definition, negotiated.)

fatal strangulation death

(*Fatal* means "causing death." Strangulation always results in death.)

forcible rape

(All rape, by definition, is forcible. Unless you are making the legal distinction between *rape* and *statutory rape,* this phrase is redundant.)

end result

(*Result,* by definition, is the end consequence.)

incumbent officeholder

(The definition of *incumbent* is officeholder.)

Beware of unnecessary modifiers. We have already discussed the problem of creating redundancies by tacking intensifiers onto already "intense" words. Another problem is tacking comparatives or superlatives onto words that do not need them.

more parallel

(Either it is or it is not parallel.)

most unique

(*Unique* means "one of a kind.")

more universal
more universally accepted

(*Universal* means "worldwide.")

most equal

(Things are either equal or unequal.)

Other wordy, sluggish expressions have crept into journalism. Here are some of the more common ones:

AVOID	INSTEAD USE
as of now	now
at the present time	now
at this point in time	now
despite the fact that	although
due to the fact	because
during the course of	during
in regard to	about, concerning
on account of	because
seeing as how	because
the reason is because	because
the reason why	why

Certain words or phrases do nothing but take up space. *A type of, a kind of,* and *in terms of* are major offenders. So are filler words such as *aspect, element, factor, situation* and *character.* Prune your sentences of deadwood. Use words and phrases that add meaning, not verbiage.

JARGON

The first meaning of the word *jargon*, one dictionary tells us, is "the inarticulate utterances of birds; meaningless chatter." The word also means the specialized language of a trade or profession. But as journalists, we ought to take to heart that first meaning. To our audience, jargon is, more often than not, "meaningless chatter."

Scientific, technical or scholarly diction insulates members of a profession from the outside world, effectively excluding "non-initiated members" from what is being said. Journalists should be "jargon slayers." Our responsibility is to communicate clearly and simply to our audience. Most jargon is not communication. It's someone's attempt to muddy the waters.

This is what the president's doctor told the press:

Previously documented decrement in auditory acuity and visual refractive error corrected with contact lenses were evaluated and found to be stable.

(*Translation:* The president's hearing loss and impaired vision have not worsened.)

Here's a banker talking:

We must effect a needs assessment of the downturn in commercial lending package applications.

(Translation: We need to find out why no one is applying for loans.)

This is a scientist reporting on findings:

Despite rigid re-examination of all experimental variables, this protocol continued to produce data at variance with our subsequently proven hypothesis.

(Translation: The experiment didn't work.)

Jargon can be used to obscure ideas or to make an ordinary idea sound important. Although some scientific or scholarly jargon may have a purpose for those within the profession—a precise, technical shorthand, for example—it serves no worthy purpose in journalistic writing. It only confuses the audience and perpetuates the gap between "experts" and "laypeople."

Using jargon in journalistic stories does not make you sound impressive. On the contrary, you impress (and help) your readers by giving them lucid explanations of difficult material, not by repeating "fancy" words and phrases they do not understand.

Abide by this rule: If you do not understand it, don't pass it on to your readers.

PUTTING WORDS TOGETHER

Clear, concise, coherent writing depends on more than careful word choice. Proper placement of these words is also imperative. However, writers make several mistakes that harm the clarity of their work.

MISPLACED MODIFIERS

A misplaced modifier does not point clearly and directly to what it is supposed to modify. Readers expect the modifier to be next to or close to what is being modified.

Adverbs are the biggest problem. *Only, nearly, almost, just, scarcely, even, hardly* and *merely* must be next to—or as close as possible to—the word or words they modify. Shifting the placement of these words changes the meaning of the sentence. Consider how the meaning changes in these simple sentences according to the placement of *only*:

Only he can help you.

(No one else can help you.)

He can only help you.

(He can't do the job; he can only help *you* do the job.)

He can help only you.

(He can't help anyone else.)

Notice how the placement of *almost* in these next two sentences changes the meaning:

The negotiations almost broke down on every clause in the contract.

(The negotiations did not quite break down.)

The negotiations broke down on almost every clause in the contract.

(Just about every clause caused problems during the negotiations.)

When we speak, we often have a devil-may-care attitude toward the placement of adverbs. But placement changes meaning. Place the adverb next to the word you intend it to modify.

MISPLACED PHRASES

Like individual words, phrases should be placed next to—or as close as possible to—what they modify.

Look at the placement of the phrase "throughout the Northwest" in these two sentences:

Aluminum producers were enraged by power outages throughout the Northwest.

(The outages occurred throughout the region.)

Aluminum producers <u>throughout the Northwest</u> were enraged by power outages.

(We don't know how widespread the outages were, but throughout the
region, the producers were angry.)

Some placement problems are a little more difficult. It is not
always desirable to place a phrase next to the word it modifies.

The city council passed <u>by a 5-2 vote</u> the zoning ordinance.

Here the phrase (*by a 5-2 vote*) is placed next to the word it
modifies (*passed*), but the result is an awkward-sounding sentence. The meaning would still be clear—and the sentence would
be more graceful—if we shift placement of the phrase:

The city council passed the zoning ordinance <u>by a 5-2 vote</u>.

MISPLACED CLAUSES

Varying the placement of clauses is one way to add diversity to
your writing. But beware: Placement changes meaning. Consider these two sentences:

The amendment <u>that the committee is considering</u> will alter
the county's land-use plan.

The amendment will alter the county's land-use plan <u>that the
committee is considering</u>.

In the first sentence, the *amendment* is under consideration. In the
second example, the *plan* is under consideration.

SQUINTING MODIFIERS

A squinting modifier is a special misplaced modifier. Because of
confusing placement, the word, phrase or clause seems to point
in two directions simultaneously. The meaning of the sentence is
ambiguous. For example:

Women who swim <u>quickly</u> develop their arm muscles.

Does this sentence mean brisk *swimming* is the key to developing arm muscles or arm muscles *quickly develop* through swimming? *Quickly* "squints" both ways, making the meaning of this sentence unclear. The sentence needs to be rewritten:

When women swim quickly, they develop their arm muscles.

When women swim, their arm muscles develop quickly.

Squinting modifiers, like other misplaced modifiers, destroy coherent thought. The best remedy is a rewrite.

DANGLING MODIFIERS

A modifier "dangles" when what it is supposed to modify is not part of the sentence. For example:

To excel in writing, a good vocabulary is necessary.

The phrase "to excel in writing" does not modify anything in the sentence. The only word it could possibly modify is *vocabulary*, but this makes no sense. A *vocabulary* cannot excel in writing. The sentence needs to be revised:

To excel in writing, you need a good vocabulary.

Now the phrase correctly modifies *you*. Not only that, the revised sentence is in the active voice. The dangling modifier sentence was in the passive voice.

Here is another dangling modifier:

After training for more than a year, the event was canceled.

Clearly, the *event* did not train for more than a year. Undoubtedly, an *athlete* or *team* trained, but the sentence does not tell us that. The modifier "after training for more than a year" dangles because what it refers to is not in the sentence. A rewrite is called for:

After training for more than a year, the team learned the event was canceled.

or

> After the team members trained for more than a year, they learned the event was canceled.

Make sure the word you mean to modify is contained in the sentence. If it is not, rewrite the sentence. Coherence is at stake.

SPLIT CONSTRUCTIONS

If you separate parts of a verb, a subject from a verb or a verb from its complement, you run the risk of destroying sentence clarity and coherence.

SPLIT PARTS OF A VERB

Split verbs often lead to incoherence. In most cases, it is best to keep auxiliary verbs next to the main verb and to avoid splitting infinitives. Look what happens to sentence unity when you separate auxiliary verbs from the main verb:

> The nurses <u>have been</u> for more than six weeks <u>picketing</u> the hospital. (auxiliary and main verb split)

> The nurses <u>have been picketing</u> the hospital for more than six weeks. (improved)

The more words you place between the verb parts, the less coherent the sentence becomes:

> The planning commission <u>will</u> along with the newly appointed citizen advisory council and the city attorney <u>decide</u> the future of the housing project. (auxiliary and main verb split)

> The planning commission, the newly appointed citizen advisory council and the city attorney <u>will decide</u> the future of the housing project. (improved)

Occasionally it is acceptable—even preferable—to split a multipart verb. Almost always, the verb is split by a single word, an adverb:

> Solid waste disposal <u>has</u> always <u>been</u> a problem in Lowell.

Placing *always* between the verb parts does not hinder coherence. In fact, it adds emphasis.

Infinitives (*to be* forms of a verb) should also, in most cases, remain intact. Splitting infinitives creates awkwardness and interferes with coherent thought.

> The IRS promised <u>to</u> as soon as possible <u>make</u> the new forms available. (split infinitive)
>
> The IRS promised <u>to make</u> the new forms available as soon as possible. (improved)

Occasionally, splitting an infinitive is unavoidable. In the following sentences, splitting the infinitive actually improves the clarity of the sentence:

> The airline's losses are expected <u>to</u> more than <u>double</u> next year.
>
> (There is a split infinitive but no clarity problem.)
>
> The airline's losses are expected more than <u>to double</u> next year.
>
> (The infinitive is intact, but the sentence suffers from awkwardness and lack of clarity.)

Remember, the issue is clarity. The sentence should read smoothly and make sense. This is the ultimate test.

SPLIT SUBJECTS AND VERBS

To aid sentence clarity and to help your reader understand quickly what you are trying to say, keep the subject and verb as close as possible. Look what happens to coherence when subject and verb are interrupted by lengthy explanatory material:

> The <u>State Department</u>, following weeks of internal debate
>   (subj.)
> that resulted in the reshuffling of dozens of employees,
> <u>restructured</u> two of its bureaus.
>   (verb)

The sentence forces readers to wade through 14 words between the subject (*State Department*) and its verb (*restructured*).

Readers may have neither the time nor the inclination to wade through tangled sentence construction. If you force them to re-read a sentence for clarity, you will probably lose them. Broadcast listeners, of course, don't have the option of rereading. The broadcaster speaks the sentence, and the audience either understands or doesn't. Be kind to your audience. Keep the subject and its verb as close together as possible:

The State Department restructured two of its bureaus
    (subj.)   (verb)
following weeks of internal debate that resulted in the re-shuffling of dozens of employees.

SPLIT VERBS AND COMPLEMENTS

The simplest construction to understand is subject–verb–object. It answers the basic journalistic question: "Who did what to whom?" Just as splitting the subject (*who*) from the verb (*did what*) interferes with clarity and coherence, so too does splitting the verb (*did what*) from its complements (*to whom*). Keep the verb and its complements (object, adverb, descriptive phrase) as close together as possible. You will promote sentence unity, readability and coherence.

Citizens' groups protested Tuesday morning in front of
                 (verb)
the state senate building what they say is the undue
                                (comple-
influence of lobbyists on legislative action.
           ment)

This sentence makes readers wait nine words until they discover what the citizens' groups were protesting. The sentence is also clumsy. To avoid losing coherent thought—and your audience—rewrite:

Citizens' groups protested what they say is the undue influ-ence of lobbyists on legislative action. Assembling in front of the state senate building Tuesday morning, they . . .

Making Sense

Every good grammatical decision you make contributes to clarity, conciseness and coherence. Choosing strong, precise words is the first step. Placing these words correctly is next. Creating parallel structure, keeping verbs in the same tense and voice, avoiding sentence fragments and rewording run-on sentences are also important elements of clarity, conciseness and coherence.

Parallel Structure

When you place like ideas in like grammatical patterns, you create parallel structure. As we discussed in Chapter 4, parallel structure lines up related ideas and offers them to the reader through the repetition of grammatical structure. It is vital to both clarity and unity. To create parallel structure using single words, you use a series of words that are the same part of speech. For example:

> Employees say the new manager is <u>forceful</u>, <u>honest</u> and <u>energetic</u>.

The related ideas are the qualities of the new manager. The grammatical pattern is the repetition of single adjectives.

To create parallel structure using phrases, repeat the pattern of the phrase. For example:

> All three candidates vowed to <u>decrease property taxes</u>, <u>increase social services</u> and <u>attract new industry</u>.

Notice that the three phrases repeat the same grammatical pattern: verb-adjective-noun. The sentence is parallel. A series of clauses can also be placed in like grammatical patterns:

> <u>When you appeal to the people</u>, <u>when you explain the problem</u>, <u>when you offer creative solutions</u>—that's when you get support, Brown told the crowd.

Parallel structure binds ideas and enhances your audience's understanding of each idea by creating a lucid pattern. If you begin a sentence using parallel structure and then break the implicit contract you have made with your audience, you create confusion and disharmony.

Parallel structure is commonly used to introduce complementary, contrasting or sequential ideas. The relationship between the ideas can be implied (as in the examples offered thus far), or it can be tagged by certain signal words. For example:

Complementary relationship: Both/and, not only/but also
Contrasting relationship: Either/or, neither/nor
Sequential relationship: First/second/third

Both heavy snowfall **and** holiday traffic will make mountain passes dangerous this weekend, say state police.

(complementary relationship, parallel structure)

Either we enforce the clean air standards or we negate the advances of the last 10 years, Brown warned yesterday.

(contrasting relationship, parallel structure)

First, turn down your thermostat; **second,** insulate your water heater; **third,** weatherstrip your windows.

(sequential relationship, parallel structure)

Whether you make the relationship explicit by using signal words or implicit by letting the ideas speak for themselves, parallel structure is vital.

SHIFTS IN TENSE AND VOICE

Unnecessary shifts in verb tense and improper shifts in verb voice are more than grammatical errors. They are mistakes that rob sentences of unity, consistency and coherence. Chapter 4 discusses tense and Chapter 6 discusses voice. Let's briefly review.

TENSE SHIFTS

Verbs not only indicate *what* action is taking place but also state—by their tense—*when* the action is taking place. Inconsistent use of tenses interferes with the reader's understanding of time sequence. Shifts in tense are necessary when you want to indicate a shift in time. But unnecessary shifts contribute to incoherent and confusing writing.

Observe these rules:

- **When the action takes place at the same time, use the same verb tense.**

    The car <u>veered</u> off the road, <u>crashed</u> through the guardrail and <u>rolled</u> down the embankment.

    (Past tense is used consistently.)

- **When you want to show a historical progression of action, shift tenses accordingly.**

    The president <u>announced</u> yesterday he <u>will be leaving</u> for Latin America next month.

    (This shift from past to future correctly indicates shift in time.)

VOICE SHIFTS

The voice of the verb shows the relationship between the doer and the action. In the active voice, the doer acts. In the passive voice, the doer is acted upon.

    The Senate passed the tax package. (active voice)

    The tax package was passed by the Senate. (passive voice)

Active voice emphasizes the doer of the action (*the Senate*). Passive voice emphasizes the recipient of the action (*the tax package*). If you shift the voice, you shift the focus of the sentence. Not only do you create an awkward sentence but you also confuse the reader.

    The Senate passed the tax package, but the arms agreement was tabled. (shift from active to passive)

    The Senate passed the tax package but tabled the arms agreement. (consistent use of active voice)

Do not shift from one voice to another. It shatters sentence unity and destroys coherence.

As you will remember from Chapter 3, a fragment is a group of words that lacks a subject, a predicate, a complete thought or any combination of the three. Grammatically, a fragment cannot stand alone. When your readers see a group of words beginning with a capital letter and ending with a period, they expect a complete thought. If instead you offer them a fragment, you confuse them. Unintentional fragments hinder both coherence and clarity.

> Parking continues to be a problem on campus.
> <u>Although two new lots have been constructed</u>.
> (fragment)

The fragment in the preceding example obscures clarity. Perhaps the writer meant:

> Although two new lots have been constructed, parking continues to be a problem on campus.

Maybe the writer intended no such connection. Perhaps the fragment was supposed to signal the beginning of a new idea:

> Parking continues to be a problem on campus. Although two new lots have been constructed, they are too far from major campus activities to be of much use, say critics.

Fragments leave your readers hanging, forcing them to guess your intended meaning. Offer your readers clear, concise, complete thoughts.

RUN-ON SENTENCES

A run-on sentence is composed of two, three or any number of whole, complete sentences. Chapter 3 discusses the run-on sentence as a grammatical problem. Here we want to emphasize it as an obstacle to concise and coherent writing.

The two most common run-on varieties are sentences inappropriately linked with *and* and sentences incorrectly spliced with commas. Both can confuse and frustrate the reader.

The regional power cooperative announced a 60 percent increase in electricity rates **and** rates for Dayton residents will double next month. (run-on sentence)

When you use *and* to link two independent clauses, you are saying the two thoughts reinforce each other or they follow each other sequentially. If neither is the case, as in the preceding example, you have created not just a run-on but also an incoherent sentence. If the thoughts are not related, rewrite the run-on as two separate sentences. If the thoughts are related, use a connecting word to signal the correct relationship.

Because the regional power cooperative announced a 60 percent increase in electricity rates, rates for Dayton residents will double next month. (improved)

When commas link clauses, readers expect the words following a comma to add to or complement what they have just read. If the clauses are not related in this way, the result is an incoherent run-on.

Terrorist activities forced closure of several major airports this summer, tourists stayed away in droves, officials quickly announced the implementation of strict anti-terrorist measures. (run-on)

This sentence needs to be rewritten. The relationship between the clauses must be expressed clearly. Commas are the wrong signals. In the absence of correct signals, it is unclear exactly what relationship exists. For example, the writer could have meant:

Because terrorist activities forced closure of several major airports this summer, tourists stayed away in droves. Officials reacted quickly by announcing the implementation of strict anti-terrorist measures. (improved)

Or:

Terrorist activities forced closure of several major airports this summer. Although officials quickly announced the implementation of strict anti-terrorist measures, tourists still stayed away in droves. (improved)

Clarity, Conciseness, Coherence

As a journalist, you must write to be read. Your thoughts must be clear; your sentences must be understandable. Clarity, conciseness and coherence begin with individual word choice. From then on, every grammatical decision you make either enhances or detracts from this triple goal. Imprecision, clutter, misplaced phrases and murky construction have no place in good writing. The goal is precise, succinct, powerful communication. It is not an easy goal. But it is an attainable one.

Style

Beyond clarity, conciseness and coherence is *style*—the selection of detail, choice of words, structure of language and pacing that make your writing uniquely yours. Style is something writers work on—and work toward—all of their professional lives. Not the private domain of fiction writers and essayists, style has an important place in journalistic writing.

Novice journalists, and many experienced ones as well, harbor several *misconceptions* about style:

- They believe if they write *lean, uncluttered* prose their writing will lack style.
- They think style has something to do with *verbal gaudiness* and *ornamental language.*
- They fear that style, because it is truly hard to define, is therefore *mysterious* and *unattainable.*

They're wrong on all three counts.

Style emerges from—and cannot exist without—crisp, lean language use. First come the fundamentals: *strong verbs, grammatical consistency, tightly constructed sentences.* Then comes style. Novelist John Updike looks at style by comparing the process of writing to the process of becoming a musician. Musicians begin by learning to identify and play individual notes. They learn how to read music. They practice scales. They play simple compositions. Only after mastering these fundamentals can they begin to develop their own manner of musical expression, their own style. Writers too must master the basics before they attempt to find their own "voice."

Journalist, editor and author William Zinsser likes to think of writers as carpenters. First, writers must learn to "saw wood neatly" and "drive nails." Later they can "bevel the edges." A beveled edge (style) is pretty, but if the structure isn't built right (constructed grammatically), it will collapse.

Writers as musicians, writers as carpenters—the message is the same. First, learn the *craft* of writing; then, explore the *art*. Precise, grammatical language does not stand in the way of stylistic writing; it is the *basis* for stylistic writing.

Style is not one particular device or "trick" but the sum of a series of careful, purposeful choices. *Liveliness*, an important element in style, is the product of crisp, direct language use. Strong, precise words; lean, uncluttered prose; and active voice all contribute to writing that moves along at a good clip.

Originality is another element of style. Journalistic information-gatherers who are keen observers, thorough researchers and astute interviewers will gather fresh and original material. Writing with style means knowing how to get the most out of this material. Choosing detail, avoiding clichéd expressions and trite images and, when appropriate, playing with words all contribute to freshness and originality.

Style also depends on an appreciation of the *cadence, rhythm* and *sound* of language. Words march to a beat. Writers can quicken or slow the pace by manipulating sentence length and sentence structure. Repetition can add accent and meter. Parallelism can add power. Words chosen for their sounds, as well as their meaning, can add unexpected spark.

Finding your own voice or style is a lifelong process. It is something to think about and aim for as you master the fundamentals of good writing on which it is based. Stylistic writing and journalistic writing are compatible. Your stories will be more forceful, more involving—and more readable—if you write with verve.

Journalism can be "literature in a hurry." It's up to you.

PART TWO

A Topical Guide to Word Use and Grammar

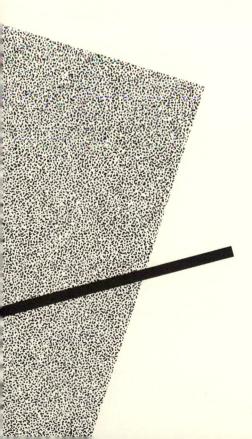

Journalists always fight the clock, but they also battle a more formidable foe: *lack of precision*. Faulty decisions about word use and grammar attack the credibility of journalists and erode their command of language. In such a struggle, journalists' best ally is correct, well-focused usage.

Word-use faults can range from the hilarious malaprop ("She wore a dress of *sequence*" instead of *sequins*) to bold editorializing with euphemisms (such as the daily newspaper that refers to Central American "Contra" forces as "freedom fighters" in news columns). While most journalists are quick to spot such obvious flaws, it is sadly apparent that specific meanings of many ordinary words are being lost or ignored. Daily problems with such words as *affect/effect, convince/persuade* and *fewer/less* illustrate why journalists must preserve the distinctions in our language.

In an effort to explain and reinforce these important meanings, Part Two of this book provides an alphabetical reference to frequently abused words and to common grammatical problems.

It is organized the way most news stories are—summaries of main points first and details later. This list of topics reflects our view of the most common areas of inquiry and misuse in word use and grammar today. Basic summaries of these points are given in this section. Details on these topics are found in Part One; often a Part Two entry will provide a page number for further reference.

Making pronouncements about the standards of usage and grammar is a risky business. But they must be made. Theodore Bernstein warns of "the twisting of our language, which is being encouraged by linguists and teachers who find it easier to follow their sometimes benighted charges than to lead them" ("The Careful Writer," p. ix). Although we recognize the dynamic nature of our language and the influence of culture, media and government on it, we nonetheless affirm the need for caution, conservatism and care.

Regulation is needed to preserve the distinctive meanings of words, so that a writer's intent is clear. Communication cannot survive under anarchy.

The guide that follows is by no means complete. Although we have never seen one that is, we have refined and increased entries from the first edition. We present it in the hope that it will help answer most of the word-use and grammar questions you face daily in journalism.

active voice/passive voice   *Voice* refers to the form of a verb as it relates to its subject. When the subject of the sentence *performs the action* ("The Second Fidelity Bank ceased operation"), the verb (*ceased*) is in the active voice. If the subject *receives the action* of the verb ("The suspects were caught in the hospital's laundry room"), the verb (*were caught*) is in the passive voice. Generally the active voice is stronger and more direct than the passive. Too much dependence on the passive voice can rob your sentence of needed strength. It may also cover up a poor reporting job. However, there are reasons to use the passive, especially when you need to stress the receiver of action rather than the performer. See Chapter 6 for a complete discussion of voice.

adverse/averse   Although these adjectives sound alike, they have distinct meanings. *Adverse,* which means "unfavorable or hostile," is used best when it modifies an adjacent noun that refers to a thing or concept:

> The doctors had not anticipated his <u>adverse</u> reaction to the medication.

However, if you want to describe someone's reluctance to do something, you should use *averse:*

> Willie Sutton never was <u>averse</u> to opening other people's safes.

affect/effect   A pox on this pair! The improper selection of one for the other is one of the most common writing faults today. There seem to be two reasons for the confusion about these words: (1) They sound alike, and (2) some writers don't understand what part of speech each is. If you remember that *affect* is almost always a *verb* that means "to influence or to pretend to have," you can see how different it is from *effect*, which is almost always a *noun* that means "result." Examples:

> The administration's program will <u>affect</u> millions of welfare recipients. (verb: "to influence")

> The defendant <u>affected</u> a carefree manner.

> (verb: "to pretend to have")

The senator questioned the <u>effect</u> of the defense cutback.

(noun: "result")

Effect is occasionally used as a verb in formal writing to mean "to bring about."

Top management <u>effected</u> some personnel changes.

You see this in stuffy business writing; it is inappropriate for journalistic writing. *Affect* can be a noun in very narrow usage, to denote certain behavior in psychology. Forget both of these uses unless you need to use and explain them in a direct quote. We don't want to sound too dogmatic about a language that should be flexible, but we think it's warranted in this case. Need a verb? Think *a*—for *affect*. Need a noun? Think *e*—for *effect*. (How are the effects of all this grammar and word–use discussion affecting you so far?)

-*aholic* endings Proof that language indeed "lives," *-aholic* words have just recently entered our vocabulary. Through slang usage *-aholic* tacked onto the end of a word has come to mean "one obsessed by," as in *workaholic* and *chocaholic*. Presumably, these new words owe their existence to *alcoholic*. But instead of taking the accepted suffix *ic*, meaning "of or pertaining to," from the root word *alcohol,* whoever created these new words stole (and misspelled) another syllable and a half. That this linguistic configuration makes no sense bothers only purists. The rest of us enjoy new words with distinct meanings.

aid/aide *Aides* ("assistants") give *aid* ("help, assistance") to their bosses. *Aid* also can be a verb, but *aide* can only be a noun.

all/any/most/some These can be singular and plural. If the word carries the meaning of "general amount or quantity," the meaning is singular:

<u>All</u> of the <u>contraband</u> was seized at the port.

<u>Some</u> of the <u>testimony</u> was striken from the record.

If you can read "individual and number" into the sentence, the plural verb should be used.

All of the <u>passengers</u> were rescued.

Have <u>any</u> of their <u>relatives</u> been notified?

See p. 62 and the entry for *none*.

allude/elude   Their meanings shouldn't *elude* you. If you are making an "indirect reference" to something, you *allude* to it. (If you want to mention it directly, you *refer* to it.)

The candidate <u>alluded</u> to the checkered business career of his opponent.

Elude is your choice if you mean "to escape or avoid detection."

The fugitive <u>eluded</u> the deputies and their dogs.

among/between   These two prepositions will probably always confuse us. In our reverie about the simple days of grade school, we sometimes recall this bit of errant dogma: *Among* relates to more than two persons or things, and *between* applies to only two. We soon discovered, of course, that nothing in life could be that simple. The archaic meaning of *between* was "by the twain," or "by two." It implies separation or connection involving two entities. *Among* implies a "distribution" involving greater, generally undefined numbers. The rule today is this: If there is a "definite relation" involved, *between* is preferred, no matter what the number.

<u>Between</u> you and me, this contract is never going to be signed.

Negotiations have broken down <u>between</u> the government mediator, auto workers and management.

Among is properly used where there is no explicit relationship stated and when distribution is stressed.

The handbills were passed out <u>among</u> the crowd.

The reward money was divided <u>among</u> the four families who supplied clues to the police department.

Chances are you'll be using *between* more than *among* in your writing. One other point about these prepositions: Remember that if they are used in a simple prepositional phrase, their objects and personal pronouns will be in the objective case. For more on this, see p. 81.

antecedents   Often hiding in sentences like snakes in tall grass, these words are reference points for the pronouns that follow.

> This is the kind of tax bill that makes investors cry.
> (antec.)   (pron.)

Because the antecedent of a pronoun sometimes is unclear, writers may have problems with number and person agreement. In the following sentences, proper antecedents are underlined:

> Sarah is one of those people who never require more than four hours' sleep.

(Why is the antecedent *people* instead of *one*? Because the sentence tells us that there is more than one person who can get by on that amount of sleep.)

> Locey is the only one of the finalists who isn't nervous.

(In this sentence, only one finalist isn't nervous, hence the singular verb.)

> Bill's theory is intriguing, but not many of his colleagues agree with it.

(The pronoun *it* properly refers to the antecedent *theory*. The intriguing theory, not Bill, is the focus here.)

Because searching for proper antecedents sometimes can be difficult, writers should take special care that the pronoun-antecedent relationship is clear.

a number of/the number of   The intended number of these phrases depends on a simple article. If the article is *a,* the meaning is plural:

> A number of senators have left the assembly.

If the article is *the,* the meaning is more indefinite and therefore is singular:

The number of tornadoes in the Midwest has declined in recent years.

These phrases illustrate an easy-to-remember tip about subject-verb agreement: If the phrase or word denotes "a general amount or quantity," the verb is singular; if the phrase or word denotes "a more definable number of individuals," the verb is plural. See p. 59.

anxious/eager   This choice causes more anxiety than eagerness. It shouldn't if you remember that you can only be anxious *about* something; you cannot be anxious *to do* that thing. *Anxious* implies fear and worry.

> The mayor said she was anxious about the outcome of this election.

If you are stimulated and excited at the prospect of doing something, then you are *eager* to do it.

> The court appointee said he was eager to deal with the pile of appeal requests on his desk.

appositive   This is a word, phrase or clause placed in the same grammatical relationship as the word that precedes it. Words in apposition have a "side-by-side" relationship. They are important to identify because they have some bearing on punctuation and case decisions. For example, a *restrictive appositive* is one that is essential to the meaning of a sentence and thus requires no commas:

> My friend John helped write headlines while his friend
> (appositive)
> Susan did the layout.
> (appositive)
>
> (A comma would not be correct after *friend* because *John* and *Susan* are essential to the meaning of the predicate nominative *friend*.)

A *non-restrictive* appositive still has a side-by-side relationship, but its meaning is not essential to the sentence. It must be set off by commas:

Bird, <u>a proven clutch player</u>, has a secure place on the roster.
(appositive)

as if/like   Advertising slogans to the contrary, don't look for the preposition *like* to join the lofty company of the conjunction. *As if* is properly used as a *conjunction* if it introduces a clause:

It looks <u>as if</u> it will rain.

Like takes a simple object; it cannot introduce a clause:

It looks <u>like</u> rain.

Some grammarians say that *like* is evolving into a conjunction. We hope that will be an extraordinarily long process.

as/than   They can be both prepositions and conjunctions. This can cause problems with case selection. If these words are used as *conjunctions*, most likely they are used to make comparisons. If so, the *nominative case* of the pronoun is needed.

There's none more handsome <u>than he</u>.

("Than he is handsome" is understood as the second clause.)

You, as well <u>as I</u>, understand the significance of this event.

However, *as* and *than* also can be *prepositions*.

Why did you pick Harold rather <u>than her</u>?

Do you really think you can pose <u>as me</u> in the inaugural parade?

Obviously, no comparisons are being made here. The pronouns following these prepositions must be in the *objective case*.

as well as   This phrase, which connects a subordinate thought to the main one, can cause agreement problems between subject and verb. Remember that the main subject—not any word or phrase parenthetical to it—controls the number and person of the verb.

The <u>house</u>, as well as its contents, <u>was</u> destroyed in the early morning fire.

<u>I</u>, as well as you, <u>am</u> facing an expensive lawsuit.

Similar parenthetical phrases are *together with, in addition to* and *along with*. You'll find it easier to isolate the true subject of the sentence if you set off these phrases with commas. See p. 57.

bad/badly Don't feel *bad* if you use these words *badly. Bad* is an *adjective*. In linking verb constructions in which you want to describe the subject, *bad* is the correct choice.

Mayor Matott said he <u>felt</u> <u>bad</u> about the report of
              (l.v.) (adj.)
campaign irregularities.

In that sentence, you are describing the mayor's state of being, not his physical ability to feel. When you describe some quality of the verb instead of the subject, you use the *adverb badly.*

The prime minister <u>took</u> her defeat <u>badly</u>.
           (verb)   (adv.)
(Badly describes the verb, not the prime minister.)

because of/due to You should always use *because of* when matching cause to effect. It is used when the writer can ask *why* in a sentence.

The stock market fell <u>because of</u> panic selling.

<u>Because of</u> an increase in wholesale prices for mozzarella cheese, the Giusti Company was forced to increase the cost of its pizzas.

Due to should never be used in anything but a linking verb construction. *Due* is an adjective; its preposition *to* relates to the condition of a subject.

The stock market drop <u>was due</u> to panic selling by nervous
             (l.v.)(adj.)
speculators.

You'll note that you can't ask *why* in this type of construction. But you can in the next sentence, and that is why *due to* is incorrect:

(Due to/<u>Because of</u>) the budget shortfall this year, no new grant applications will be accepted.

beside/besides *Beside* means "next to" or "at the side of." *Besides* means "in addition to."

The wary guard stood <u>beside</u> the visiting dignitary.
    (next to)

<u>Besides</u> Harry and me, only Sarah knew of the escape plan.
(in addition to)

Remember that simple objects of these prepositions take the objective case.

bi-/semi- *Bi-* means "two," and *semi-* means "half." This distinction works fine until you come to *years*.

bimonthly—every two months

semimonthly—twice a month

If you mean something that happens twice a year, use *semiannual* rather than *biannual*, even though the dictionary recognizes both. That will avoid confusion with *biennial* (something that happens every two years). Note that the prefixes *bi-* and *semi-* are hyphenated only when the word that follows them begins with an *i* or is capitalized.

both/few/many/several These indefinite pronouns always take a plural verb. See p. 61.

brand names/trademarks These are business-created words that have not fallen into generic usage. Do you really want to refer to a specific product, or do you just want to mention the *process?* If you want to mention the process or the generic name, avoid brand name reference. Do not write, for example,

The spy <u>xeroxed</u> all the documents.

For one thing, *Xerox,* a registered trade name, isn't a verb; the spy can photocopy the documents, but he or she can't *xerox, canonize* or *savinize* them. Other examples are *Scotch* tape (a brand of cellophane tape), *Coke* (one of many cola beverages), *Mace* (a brand of tear gas) and *Kleenex* (a brand of facial tissue). All brand names and trademarks should be capitalized.

bureaucratese/jargon   They give proof that our language is dynamic, although somewhat inefficient. These words and phrases, used by government workers, sports writers, scientists, doctors, computer programmers and a host of other professionals, have changed our language—but not for the better. Often, they have only weakened the economy of our writing. You no longer measure the effect of contingency spending on a budget; you ascertain how the program will *impact* on fiscal planning. You no longer evaluate things; you effect a *needs assessment.* You no longer say now or today; it is *at this point in time.* A heart attack becomes an *M. I.* (myocardial infarct). A stroke becomes a *C. V. A.* (cerebral vascular accident). A basketball team doesn't defeat another one; it *rips, tears, repels, devours (dices, peels, juliennes?)* the visiting Tigers, Spartans or what have you. Perhaps the culprit is poor word selection. Using words that reflect our trendiness, our desire to be at the vanguard of new expressions, creates a barrier for clear communication. These words sock in the borders of our expression with a fog of our own making.

but   It is most frequently a conjunction. It connects words and phrases of equal rank and implies a *contrast* between those elements. It almost always requires a comma between the clauses it separates.

> The commissioners approved the budget resolution, but they denied a room tax provision for that document.

But also can be a preposition meaning "except."

> Everybody but me went to the party.

Note that the objective case is required for the pronoun when it relates to the preposition.

Can *but* be used to begin a sentence, like the conjunctive adverb *however*? Of course, if you don't overdo it. Just remember it's meant to coordinate clauses. But who are we to be so dogmatic about grammar?

can/may   Preserve their distinctiveness if you can! *Can* denotes ability, and *may* denotes *possibility and permission*. In question form, *may* is almost always your choice:

> May I go to the exhibit?

"*Can* he go to the exhibit?" has nothing to do with his *ability* to do anything, although "Do you think I *can* win this election?" is correct usage because it asks for confidence in one's ability to do something. This, too, would be correct:

> She can run the 200-meter dash faster than any of her teammates.

Some stylists have thrown in the towel on the interchangeability of *can* and *may*. Don't give up on these two; they're worth the fight. Postscript: Remember that *may* also can express possibility.

> I may buy that new boat we've been talking about.

careen   This word often falls victim to imprecise usage. Unless it is leaning sideways or tossing about like a boat under sail, a car that is out of control doesn't *careen* into a crowd of shoppers. It might speed, skid or veer, but it rarely will take a nautical lean, balancing nicely on two wheels en route to an insurance claim.

case   Understanding case helps explain why *who* rather than *whom, us* rather than *we,* and *s'* are needed in certain sentences. The three cases are nominative, objective and possessive. Certain pronouns change their form to accommodate a change in case, and nouns change only in their possessive case. See Chapter 5.

censor/censure   These words both perform negative, though different, actions. You can *censor* materials by screening, changing or forbidding them.

The press officer <u>censored</u> all dispatches from the embassy.

You generally can only *censure* people—by condemning them or expressing disapproval of their actions.

The senators <u>censured</u> their colleague because he attempted to <u>censor</u> the minutes of his committee.

These words can also be nouns. They sound like *censer* (a container used to burn incense) and *sensor* (a photoelectric cell).

chair/chairperson   Despite protestations of old-line grammarians who cry tradition and purity, we feel the term *chairman* unfairly and incorrectly assumes maleness of that position. It is one of many such terms in our language. For years, authoritative dictionaries have referred to *chair* as "a person who presides over a meeting" and "an office or position of authority." A person— man or woman—can *chair* a meeting or can be a program *chair*. It assumes nothing but the position itself. Because the words seem contrived and awkward, avoid *chairer* and *chairperson*. However, some news organizations now are using the official title of the position in their stories, no matter how awkward it may seem. See generic agreement, p. 69.

clause   This is a group of words that contains both a subject and a verb. Although that may sound like the definition of a sentence, not all clauses are complete thoughts. *Independent clauses* express complete thoughts and can stand alone as sentences.

The California <u>Supreme Court</u> <u>handed</u> Democrats a major
           (subj.)   (verb)
victory yesterday . . .

Dependent clauses have subjects and verbs, but their meaning is incomplete because they may contain a relative pronoun that traces its meaning to the independent clause.

. . . <u>that</u> should <u>guarantee</u> them a majority in the House.
(rel. pron.)   (verb)

So we have one sentence with two clauses. Rather than creating two sentences, a writer may choose to keep a principal thought in one construction by making one thought dominant (independent) and the other subordinate (dependent). See p. 37.

clutter   This is the excess baggage that obscures clarity in writing. With clutter, thoughts are unfocused. Phrase is tacked onto phrase, forcing clauses into a line of uneven thought. Packing too much into a sentence—something that happens often in writing a summary news lead—produces clutter:

> A spectator knifed the referee to death after a soccer match at Bosanski Milosevac, near Modrica in Central Yugoslavia, the Belgrade tabloid *Vecernje Novosti* reported Saturday.

Simpler sentences and shorter paragraphs can reduce clutter:

> Is one player strong enough to lift a team to the top of the college basketball world?
>   Perhaps—if his name is Sampson.

Eliminating clutter doesn't have to result in bland, simple-minded writing.

collective nouns   Their singular forms denote a group of people or things—for example, *jury, herd, athletics* and *politics.* They can be troublesome for subject-verb agreement. If the noun is considered as a whole, the verb and associated pronouns are singular:

> The <u>jury</u> <u>has returned</u> with <u>its</u> verdict.

If that unit is broken up or considered individually, the plural verb is used:

> The <u>herd</u> of cattle have scattered because of the dust storm.

Although the preceding sentence is correct, it sounds awkward because of the idea of herd. If the cattle were split up, they are not the same herd. It would sound better to write, "The *cattle* have scattered. . . ." See p. 62.

collision   This is a violent contact between *moving* bodies. An accident between a moving car and a stationary telephone pole is not a collision; it is a crash. An oil tanker does not collide with a bridge. In a more figurative sense, ideas, opinions and, yes, words can collide.

colon   This punctuation mark (:) introduces thoughts, quotations or series. Capitalize matter following a colon only if it can stand alone as a sentence.

> His parting thought to the committee would haunt them for many years: You can't build a tax base on deficit spending.

but

> Besides cartooning, Charles Schulz has one great passion: hockey.

comma splice   This is also known as *comma fault*. It occurs at two levels of composition. It may be a mistake by the careless writer who joins two independent clauses without either a coordinating conjunction or a semicolon. Or it may be a device by the accomplished writer who does not want the harsh stop of a semicolon to slow the meter of a sentence. These are unacceptable comma splices:

> The council approved the resolution, the mayor vetoed it the next day.

(The sentence lacks the conjunction *but* or a semicolon between clauses.)

> He enjoys reviewing movies, however, he says he can't waste his time on "trash like this."

(Presence of the conjunctive adverb *however* requires a semicolon between clauses—that is, between *movies* and *however*.)

In short sentences, the comma splice has received the blessing of most grammarians. *"You'll like her, she's an Aquarius"* can survive without a conjunction or semicolon. Like the sentence fragment, the comma splice should be used sparingly—and by writers who know when they are using it!

compared to/compared with These are about as interchangeable as American and European electric voltage. When you liken one thing to another, you must use *compared to:*

> The governor compared the logging of pristine, old-growth timber <u>to</u> taking a thoroughbred racehorse and chopping it into dog meat.

When you place items side by side to examine their similarities and differences, you must use *compared with:*

> The interest rate is 5.5 percent, compared <u>with</u> 1979's rate of 14.5 percent.

As you can see, the use of *compared to* is figurative and metaphorical. Not so *compared with*—it's statistical rather than creative. Whereas you might compare today's weather *to* a joyous song of hope, you can examine facts and compare last winter's rainfall *with* the winter rain in 1928.

complement/compliment They both can be nouns or verbs. *Complement* is defined as "that which completes something, supplements it, or brings it to perfection." That is quite different from *compliment*, which means "an expression of praise or admiration." So, a hat may complement a suit, but you would compliment the wearer on his or her hat.

compose/comprise *Compose* is not as direct as *comprise*. Something is composed of other things (made up of); however, one thing comprises (takes in, includes) other things. The following are *correct* usages:

> The salad dressing was <u>composed of</u> olive oil, vinegar and spices.

> Her speech <u>comprised</u> four major themes.

As you can see from the last example, the whole (*speech*) comprises the parts (*themes*). A whole is never *comprised of* the parts. That would be the same as saying "The whole is included of its parts."

Another way of looking at *comprise* is to think of it as embracing something, as in

> The chief justice's opinion <u>comprised</u> issues of privacy, false light and appropriation.

With all this said, it must be added that *comprise* is not a word we would use more than occasionally. Sometimes it just doesn't sound right!

compound modifiers   These are two adjectives or an adverb joined with an adjective to modify a noun. Often a hyphen is needed to "join" these modifiers, to make the meaning clear:

> <u>mud-covered</u> boat   <u>well-intentioned</u> meaning
>
> <u>hard-driving</u> perfectionist

Columnist James J. Kilpatrick spotted this advertisement in a Midwestern newspaper; its lack of hyphens made it read like a news report of an industrial accident:

> "Chef cut self basting turkeys"

Of course, the ad was trying to sell *Chef-cut, self-basting* turkeys.
Modifiers do not require a hyphen if they are preceded by *very* or an *-ly* adverb. These adverbs obviously modify what follows, and there is no mistaking their intention:

> <u>highly acclaimed</u> production   <u>very enthusiastic</u> student

Don't string too many modifiers together in the name of description and economy. You may just get clutter.

continual/continuous   *Continual* means "repeated or intermittent," and *continuous* means "unbroken."

> Must I suffer your <u>continual</u> interruptions?
> Under the spell of the heat and his thirst, the legionnaire imagined he saw a <u>continuous</u> line of canteens stretched across the horizon.

convince/persuade   If you think these words are identical in meaning, we're just going to have to persuade you that they're not. We'll do that until you're convinced! To begin with, people *do not* convince others of anything; that *action* is called *persuasion*.

> The committee <u>persuaded</u> the mayor to run for re-election.

To be *convinced* is to exist in a *state* in which one feels secure in a decision or a principle. It is always an adjective, not a verb.

> The mayor is <u>convinced</u> she can win another term.

If a person attempts to persuade another and is successful, the first person is thought of as persuasive. Obviously, the argument has been convincing. The process is to persuade; the hoped-for result is to be convinced. Got that now? You cannot be convinced to do anything. You can be convinced that something is right or convinced of its correctness. Convinced? Or do you need to be persuaded?

dangling modifiers   A modifier dangles when it does not modify anything in the sentence. For example:

> <u>Facing indictment for income tax evasion</u>, the city council rescinded his appointment.

The participial phrase *facing indictment for income tax evasion* has nothing to modify. The first referent we see is *council*. It stretches both imagination and credulity to think the entire city council is under indictment. The only other possible referent is *appointment*, but this makes no sense. Poor sentence construction has buried the true referent—the person who is facing indictment. The sentence needs to be rewritten:

> Facing indictment for income tax evasion, <u>Smith</u> was ousted by the city council.

The participial phrase now has a referent, *Smith.*

Dangling modifiers most often occur at the beginnings of sentences. Although they tend to be verbals—participial phrases, gerund phrases and infinitive phrases—appositives, clauses and simple adjectives can dangle as well. The test is whether the person or thing being modified by the word, phrase or clause is in the sentence. Dangling modifiers destroy logical, coherent thought. Rewrite or revise the sentence to include the missing referent. See p. 151.

dash   An enticing piece of punctuation because of its informality, directness and drama, the dash (—) is often used excessively and incorrectly. Journalists should consider routinely using commas, colons and parentheses and saving dashes for special occasions. The two main uses of the dash in journalistic writing are:

1. to create drama and emphasis at the end of a sentence

> The film was beautifully photographed, superbly acted, expertly directed—and boring.

2. to clearly set off a long clause or phrase that adds information to the main clause

> "Howard the Duck"—golden boy George Lucas' one and only mistake—was a box office bomb.

Use dashes for abrupt breaks and added emphasis. Remember that excessive use robs the dash of its power.

data and other foreign plurals   Many English words have their roots in Latin; some are derived from Greek. Some of these words conform to singular-plural rules unlike our own. *Data, media* and *alumni* are commonly used Latin plurals. If you mean a single piece of information, use *datum* (although that would admittedly be rare). Magazines are one *medium;* radio and TV are broadcast *media.* The word *alumni* presents further complications: A group of men and women who have graduated from a school are *alumni;* one male graduate is an *alumnus;* one female grad is an *alumna.* And to be perfectly correct, a group of female grads would be *alumnae.* The Greek words *criteria* and *phenomena* are plural. Their singulars are *criterion* and *phenomenon.*

Data can be a difficult word in subject-verb agreement. It almost always is considered a unit, even though its form is plural. In this case, it is considered a collective noun and should take a singular verb:

Your data <u>is</u> invalid. (unit)

However, if the sense of data is individual items, use a plural verb:

The data <u>were</u> collected from seven tracking sites.
(individual items)

dependent clause   Although it contains both a predicate and a subject, a dependent clause does not express a complete thought and cannot stand alone as a sentence. Dependent clauses depend on main clauses for their completion.

Because the tax levy failed (dependent clause)

Because the tax levy failed, the county parks will be closed this summer. (complete sentence)

Recognizing dependent clauses will help you (1) to avoid fragments (treating dependent clauses as if they were complete sentences); (2) to vary sentence structure. Placing the dependent clause in front, in the middle or at the end of the main clause is one technique for adding diversity to sentence structure. See p. 37.

different from/different than   For those who take comfort from edicts, here's one: Use *different from* and you will never be wrong. If this leaves you wondering why *different than* exists, join the ranks of confused and contentious grammarians who have been arguing this point for years. Unless you're interested in delving into the nether regions of structural linguistics or semantic compatibility, consider using *different than* only when it introduces a *condensed clause* (a clause that omits certain words without loss of clarity).

Open meeting laws are <u>different</u> in California <u>than</u> (they are) in Oregon. (condensed clause)

With a condensed clause, *different than* saves you from a wordier— but nonetheless grammatical—construction like *from that/those which*. To avoid clutter and clumsiness, you may want to use *different than*. In general, however, play it safe with *different from*.

differ from/differ with   Politicians differ from ("are unlike") each other, but they may not differ with ("disagree with") each other. Although both phrases express contrast, they are not interchangeable. When you mean two items are dissimilar, use *differ from*. When you mean two items are in conflict use *differ with*.

> The tract houses did not <u>differ from</u> each other.
>
> The housing developers <u>differed with</u> the city zoning board.

discreet/discrete   Yes, it's true—both of these words are adjectives, and both are pronounced the same. But they do have discrete meanings! *Discreet* means prudent or careful, especially about keeping confidences, as in this sentence:

> The butler may have been stuffy, but he certainly was <u>discreet</u>.

Discrete means distinct or separate, as in this sentence:

> Negotiators consider comparable worth a <u>discrete</u> issue in the pay talks.

disinterested/uninterested   A *disinterested* ("impartial") observer may be *uninterested* ("lack interest") in the situation, but the words are not synonymous.

drug   A *drug* is any substance used as medicine in the treatment of a disease. Headline writers have made this word synonymous with *narcotics,* a particular group of sense-dulling, usually addictive drugs. All narcotics are drugs; all drugs are not narcotics. Be precise when using these words. To avoid confusion (and the possibility of libel), use *medicine* when referring to a substance used to treat a disease or injury.

each/either/neither   When used as subjects, these three pronouns always take singular verbs.

> <u>Each</u> <u>is</u> responsible for his or her own equipment.
>
> <u>Neither</u> of the defendants <u>was</u> found guilty.

When these words are used as adjectives, the nouns they modify always take a singular verb.

> Either answer is correct.
>
> Neither candidate speaks to the issues.

See p. 58.

either . . . or/neither . . . nor   Called correlative conjunctions, these word pairs (along with *both . . . and, not so . . . as, not only . . . but also*) should connect similar grammatical elements in parallel form.

> He can either pay the back taxes or a jail sentence might be imposed. (weak, lacks symmetry)
>
> He can either pay the back taxes or risk a jail sentence.
>
> (improved, parallel)

Correlative conjunctions also pose *agreement* problems. When a compound subject is linked by a correlative conjunction, the subject closest to the verb determines the number of the verb.

> Neither the legislator nor her aides were available for comment.

When the subject closest to the verb is singular, you must use a singular verb. The construction is grammatical but sometimes graceless:

> Neither the aides nor the legislator was available for comment.

Avoid awkwardness by placing the plural subject next to the verb. See p. 61.

elicit/illicit   These two words may sound alike, but the similarity stops there. *Elicit,* a verb, means to bring out or draw forth. *Illicit,* an adjective, means illegal or unlawful.

> His illicit behavior elicited strong community reaction.

enormity/enormousness   Be wary. These words are not synonymous. *Enormity* means "wickedness." *Enormousness* refers to "size."

> The enormity of his deception was not discovered for years.

> The enormousness and complexity of the problem staggered even the greatest political thinkers.

exclamation point   Expressing strong emotion or surprise, the exclamation point (!) is rarely used in journalistic writing. Its use is almost always limited to direct quotations. Remember to place the exclamation point inside the quotation marks.

> "I'll kill you when this is over!" the witness screamed at the lawyer.

farther/further   If you're a working journalist in the year 2000, you probably won't have to worry about this bothersome duo. *Farther,* say grammarians, is on the way out. But language often changes slowly, and the distinction between these two words will be with us for a while. Use *farther* to express "physical distance"; use *further* when referring to "degree, time or quantity."

> The commission recommended extending the boundaries farther.

> The commission will discuss the issue further.

feel   Save this overused word to refer to the tactile or emotional; do not use it as a synonym for "think" or "believe."

fewer/less   This is a much-abused pair, but the distinctions are simple: When you refer to a number of individual items, *fewer* is your choice; when you refer to a bulk, amount, sum, period of time or concept, use *less*.

> Fewer doctors result in less medical care.

> At Data Corporation, fewer than 10 employees make less than $50,000 a year.

In the last example, we are not talking about individual dollars, but a sum (amount) of money.

fragments An unfinished piece of a sentence, a fragment may be a single word, a phrase or a dependent clause. It may lack a subject, a predicate, a complete thought or any combination of the three. Whatever form it takes, whatever element it lacks, a fragment is not a grammatical sentence and should not stand alone. Fragments can be *rewritten* to include subject, predicate and complete thought; *incorporated* into complete sentences; or *attached* to main clauses. See p. 41.

Now you know the rule. Here's the loophole: Fragments, when used purposefully by skillful writers, constitute a stylistic technique. With their clipped, punchy beat, fragments can create excitement and grab reader attention. But this special stylistic device must be appropriate to both subject and medium and should be used sparingly.

gender-specific references (*he/she*) Language reflects culture. When a society changes, we believe language ought to keep pace. We are speaking not of faddish words or slang expressions but of the way language treats people. The language in the following sentences is no longer an accurate reflection of our society:

A <u>nurse</u> ought to be attentive to <u>her</u> patients.

A <u>state legislator</u> has a responsibility to <u>his</u> constituents.

In these sentences we see outdated sexual stereotypes—nurses are female, legislators are male. From a grammatical point of view, the problem is choosing a referent (*she, he, him, her, his, hers*) that reflects reality rather than presuming maleness or femaleness of a neuter noun. Because the singular neuter pronoun (*it, its*) cannot refer to a person, we have two grammatical options if we want to avoid sexual stereotyping:

1. Use both the masculine and the feminine pronoun when referencing a noun that could refer to either sex.

A <u>nurse</u> ought to be attentive to <u>his</u> or <u>her</u> patients.

2. Change the neuter noun to the plural and use plural neuter pronouns (*they, them, their*).

> State legislators have a responsibility to their constituents.

In your effort to treat both sexes fairly in language, don't fall prey to "political" solutions that accept errors in agreement. The following ad copy from the National Urban League uses a singular subject, singular verb and plural possessive pronoun:

> Everybody deserves to make it on their own.

This may be well-intentioned, but it does not advance the cause of non-sexist language; it abuses correct language. Two solutions are obvious:

> Everybody deserves to make it on his or her own.
>
> All people deserve to make it on their own.

See p. 69.

hanged/hung   The verb *hang* is conjugated differently depending on the object of the hanging. The conjugation *hang, hung, hung* refers to *objects*.

> The portrait hung in the museum.

The conjugation *hang, hanged, hanged* refers to *people* (executions or suicides).

> He hanged himself rather than spend his life in prison.

hopefully   Possibly the single most abused word in our language, *hopefully* means "with hope." It describes how a subject feels ("hopeful").

> Hopefully, he opened the mailbox looking for the check.

Hopefully—regardless of what you may hear or read—does not mean "it is hoped that." The following sentence is *incorrect:*

> Hopefully, the check will arrive.

The *check* is not "hopeful." *Hopefully* does not describe anything in the preceding sentence. It is, in fact, a dangling modifier. People have so thoroughly abused *hopefully* in conversational language (making it synonymous with "it is hoped") that the abuse is now part of our written language. For correctness, precision and clarity, respect the real meaning of the word. If you mean "it is hoped," write that.

hyphens A typographical bridge that links words, the hyphen (-) has three uses in journalistic writing:

1. It joins *compound modifiers* unless one of the modifiers is *very* or an *-ly* adverb. Compound modifiers are two or more adjectives or adverbs that do not separately describe the word they modify.

> a <u>well-mannered</u> child (hyphen needed)
>
> the <u>newly elected</u> senator (*-ly* adverb, no hyphen)

2. It links certain *prefixes* to the words that follow. It's best to check a dictionary or stylebook on this rule because exceptions abound. One basic guideline is this: If the prefix ends in a vowel and the next word begins with the same vowel, hyphenate (except *cooperate* and *coordinate*).

3. It links words when a *preposition* is *omitted.*

> <u>score of 5-3</u> (preposition *to* omitted)
>
> <u>June-August</u> profits (preposition *through* omitted)

See p. 119.

-ics words Words ending with the Greek suffix *-ics* (athletics, politics, graphics, acoustics, tactics, etc.) often present agreement problems. Although the final *s* makes these words *look* plural, they can be either singular or plural depending on meaning. If the word refers to "a science, art or general field of study," it is treated as *singular* and takes a singular verb. If the word refers to "the act, practices or activities" of the field, it takes a *plural* verb.

> <u>Politics is</u> a challenging career. (the field of politics, singular)
>
> His <u>politics change</u> every year. (the practice of politics, plural)

Some *-ics* words do not carry both meanings. *Hysterics,* for example, always takes the *plural* because it always refers to "acts and practices."

if I were   This common subjunctive mood construction is often mistakenly written *If I was.* But the subjunctive mood, which is used to express a non-existent, hypothetical or improbable condition, influences the form of the verb. *Were* is the subjunctive form of the verb *to be.* The following sentences are grammatically correct:

> If he <u>were</u> president, we would have a balanced budget.

> If the housing industry <u>were</u> to collapse, the local economy would soon follow.

if/whether   These conjunctions are not interchangeable. *If* means "in the event that," "granting that," "on the condition that." It is often used to introduce a *subjunctive clause* (a clause that expresses a non-existent, hypothetical or improbable condition).

> <u>If</u> Smith wins, the Democrats will have a majority.
>
> (in the event that)

> <u>If</u> the volcano were to erupt again, hundreds would have to be evacuated. (hypothetical condition)

Whether means "if it is so that," "if it happens that," or "in case." It is generally used to introduce the first of a set of possibilities.

> She asked <u>whether</u> the evidence was admissible. (if it is so)

> <u>Whether</u> he wins or loses, this will be his last campaign.
>
> (introduces a set of possibilities)

For the sake of precision and conciseness, use *whether,* not *whether or not.* The *or not* is implied. To state it is redundant.

> Whether [or not] the schools stay open depends on the fate of tomorrow's budget levy.

impact   Robbed of its power by overuse, *impact* means a "collision" or a "violent or forceful striking together." Unfortunately, writers use *impact* when they really mean something much calmer such as *effect* or *influence*.

> When her car hit the guard rail, the <u>impact</u> caused the front end to jackknife. (correct)

> No one knows what <u>impact</u> the report will have on future development. (misuse; use *effect* or *influence*)

Impact has also fallen prey to jargon mongers who now incorrectly employ it as a verb ("The televised debates *impacted* the election") or an adjective ("federally *impacted* areas"). The only thing that can be *impacted* is a tooth, and that's unpleasant enough.

imply/infer   Often confused, these verbs are not interchangeable. *Imply* means "to suggest or hint." *Infer* means "to deduce or conclude from facts or evidence."

> When he <u>implied</u> Smith was guilty, the jury <u>inferred</u> he had an ax to grind.

indefinite pronouns   Because indefinite pronouns don't always specify number (*anyone, everyone, few, some*), they can cause agreement problems. Here are a few rules to follow:

□ When used as subjects, *each, either, anyone, everyone, much, no one, nothing* and *someone* always take a singular verb.

□ Acting as subjects, *both, few, many* and *several* always take a plural verb.

□ Pronouns such as *any, none* and *some* take singular verbs when they refer to "a unit or general quantity." If they refer to "amount or individuals," they take a plural verb.

> <u>Some</u> of the construction <u>was</u> delayed (general quantity)

> because <u>some</u> of the workers <u>were</u> on strike (individuals).

See p. 21.

independent clause   Also known as the *principal* or *main clause,* an independent clause contains a subject, predicate and complete thought. When it stands alone as a grammatically complete sentence, it is called a *simple sentence*. Two independent clauses linked by a coordinating conjunction make a *compound sentence*. See p. 38.

-ing endings   A common suffix, *-ing* can be added to a verb to create the present progressive form ("She is running for office") or a verbal ("Running for office requires stamina"). It can also be added to a noun, creating a verbal that gives the noun a sense of action. *Parenting* is the action of being a *parent* (and follows the linguistic tradition of *mother/mothering*).

Although *-ing*ing a noun can be a useful device that creates new words with distinct meanings, it can also be unnecessarily trendy. Language should change in response to culture and not merely for the sake of change. For example,

Gifting is a holiday tradition

is an ugly, awkward construction. Use new *-ing* words sparingly and only when they capture a unique meaning without damaging the rhythm and sound of the language.

Initiate/instigate   At our own instigation, we have initiated an investigation of this troublesome pair. It is not correct to write, for example,

He instigated the first tapioca sculpture contest

when you mean that this deluded artist began or originated the contest. Instead, he *initiated* (began) it. This would be a proper use of *instigate:*

At great personal expense, he instigated an investigation of the Baldness Is Natural Foundation.

In this case, he did not begin the investigation—he pressed for it.

in/into   These prepositions are not interchangeable. *In* denotes location or position. *Into* indicates motion.

> The judge was <u>in</u> the courtroom. (location, position)
>
> The next witness walked <u>into</u> the courtroom. (movement)

Regardless of current slang, *into* should never be used as a substitute for "involved with" or "interested in." This colloquial use is not only sloppy but also weak and ambiguous.

> For the past year, she's been <u>into</u> swimming.
>
> (ambiguous slang)
>
> She's been swimming a mile a day for the past year.
>
> (improved)

invoke/evoke   Probably because both words contain *-voke* from the Latin root *vocare*, "to call," these very different words often get confused. *Invoke* means to appeal to or call forth earnestly. *Evoke* means to produce or elicit (a reaction, a response) or to reawaken (memories, for example).

> When the speaker <u>invoked</u> God, he <u>evoked</u> a strong reaction from his atheist audience.

irregardless   Banish this word from your vocabulary. *Regardless,* which means "without regard for" or "unmindful of" is the word you're after. The *-less* suffix creates the negative meaning. When you mistakenly add the *-ir* prefix, you create a double negative.

its/it's   *Its* is the possessive form of the neuter pronoun *it*. Do not confuse this with *it's*, which is a contraction for *it is* or *it has*.

> The committee reached <u>its</u> decision yesterday.
>
> (neuter possessive)
>
> "<u>It's</u> going to be a close vote," said Smith.
>
> (contraction for *it is*)

Use *it* or *its*—not *she* or *her*—when referring to nations or ships.

The S.S. <u>France</u> made <u>its</u> first voyage more than 20 years ago.

Mexico is carefully patrolling <u>its</u> borders.

-ize words A useful suffix, *-ize* has been employed since the time of the Greeks to change nouns into verbs (*final/finalize, burglar/burglarize*). But the *-ization* of words has now reached epidemic proportions. Writers interested in the clarity, precision and beauty of language need to take precautions. Tacking *-ize* onto the ends of nouns often creates useless, awkward and stodgy words.

IZ–
KI

The commander announced a new plan to <u>soldierize</u> the troops.

The agency may <u>permanentize</u> its position by <u>routinizing</u> its procedures.

"Verbizing" nouns is dangerous business. The result is often tongue–twisting, bureaucratic–sounding clutter. Before you use an *-ize* word, check your dictionary. Make sure the word has a unique meaning and pay attention to sound. See p. 142.

kind of/sort of Conversationally, we use *kind of* and *sort of* to mean "rather" or "somewhat":

It's <u>kind of</u> (somewhat) cloudy today.

I'm <u>sort of</u> (rather) tired.

But casual usage and clear, precise written language are often two different things. Restrict your use of *kind of* and *sort of* to mean "a species or subcategory of," as in:

This is the <u>kind of</u> development Boomtown needs.

In many cases, you can avoid the problems posed by *kind of* and *sort of* by avoiding the words themselves. Often these phrases merely take up space without adding meaning.

lay/lie *Lay,* a transitive verb, always requires a direct object. *Lie,* an intransitive verb, never takes a direct object.

> Before lying down (no direct object), she laid the book (direct object) on the table.

Be careful not to confuse *lie* and *lay* in the past tense. The past tense of *lie* is *lay*; the past tense of *lay* is *laid.*

> lie, lay, lain, lying
>
> lay, laid, laid, laying

See p. 15.

lend/loan Because *lend* has a longer history as a verb, many language experts prefer it to *loan* in written usage. But *loan,* originally a noun, has also come to mean "to lend" as a verb, and the distinction between the two words is fading. In spoken language, the distinction is almost nonexistent. Rather than worry about the differing niceties observed by various media organizations or editors, play it safe: Use *lend* as a verb and *loan* as a noun. The one exception currently favored by most experts is *loan* as a verb in financial contexts:

> The bank *loaned* Mortech $1.5 million.

less than/under Do not use *under* unless you mean "physically underneath." If you mean "a lesser quantity or amount," use *less than.*

> The county budget was under $80 million. (incorrect)
>
> The county budget was less than $80 million. (correct)

Also see the entries for *fewer/less* and *more than/over.*

linking verbs A linking verb connects a subject to an equivalent word in the sentence. That word—a predicate noun, a predicate pronoun or a predicate adjective—refers to the subject by either restating it or describing it. The principal linking verbs are *be, seem, become, appear, feel* and *look.*

LA–
LI

She <u>became</u> a best-selling <u>novelist</u>.

(*novelist,* a predicate noun, restates subject *she.*)

It <u>is</u> <u>he</u>.

(*He,* a predicate pronoun, restates the subject *it.*)

He <u>feels</u> <u>bad</u>.

(*Bad,* a predicate adjective, describes the subject *he.*)

Note that the predicate pronoun following a linking verb must be in the nominative case.

It is <u>he</u>.

not

It is <u>him</u>.

Remember that a modifier following a linking verb must be an adjective.

He feels <u>bad</u>.

not

He feels <u>badly</u>.

See the entry for *bad/badly* and pp. 12, 16 and 35.

median/average (mean)   Election results, political polls, budgets, research findings—so much of today's reporting depends on numbers and statistics that journalists ought to understand at least a few basic terms. *Median* is the middle value in a distribution of items, the point at which half of the items are above and half below. *Average* is the sum of a group of items divided by the number of items in the group. *Mean* is statisticians' talk for *average.* Statistically, they are virtually synonymous.

Number of years spent on death row by prisoners of state X:

Mr. A	18	Mr. D	10	Mr. G	6
Mr. B	14	Mr. E	7	Mr. H	6
Mr. C	10	Mr. F	6	Mr. I	4

The *median* years spent on death row is 7; that is, half of the prisoners spent more than 7 years in jail, half spent less. The *average* (or *mean*) number of years spent on death row is 9; it is the sum of all the years divided by the number of people.

misplaced modifiers   A misplaced modifier is a single word, phrase or clause that does not clearly and logically point to what it is supposed to modify. Be meticulous in your placement of modifiers. Place them next to, or as close as possible to, the word or words they describe. Misplacement not only causes confusion but also can change the meaning of the sentence.

> The committee <u>almost</u> defeated every budget item.
>
> (The adverb *almost* modifies *defeated*.)
>
> The committee defeated <u>almost</u> every budget item.
>
> (Now *almost* modifies *every*, which modifies *budget item*.)

more than/over   Like *less than* and *under,* these words are not interchangeable. Do not use *over* unless you are referring to "a spatial relationship." For "figures and amounts," the correct phrase is *more than.*

> <u>More than</u> 50 fighter planes flew <u>over</u> the desert.

none   This troublesome indefinite pronoun often causes agreement problems. Use a *singular* verb when *none* means "no one or not one." When *none* means "no two, no amount or no number," use a *plural* verb. The singular/plural choice depends on the meaning of the sentence.

> <u>None</u> ("not one") of the reporters <u>was</u> admitted to the court-room.
>
> <u>None</u> ("no amount") of the taxes <u>were</u> paid.

See the entry for *indefinite pronouns* and p. 62.

numerals   Your news organization may have specific rules concerning numerals. Check first. In the absence of other guidelines, follow these rules:

1. Spell out whole numbers below *10:* three, seven.

2. Use figures for *10* and above: 14, 305.

3. Spell out fractions less than one: two-thirds, three-quarters.

4. Spell out *first* through *ninth* when they indicate a sequence: She was first in line; the Ninth Amendment. Use figures for *10th* and above.

5. Spell out numerals at the beginning of a sentence. The only exception is a calendar-year date.

These are general rules. Your organization may have special guidelines for ages, percentages, fractions, election returns, monetary units, dimensions, temperatures or any number of special cases. The Associated Press Stylebook is a good reference.

occur/take place   Although one of the secondary definitions for *occur* is to "take place," contemporary journalistic use favors this distinction: *Occur* refers to "an accidental or unscheduled event"; *take place* refers to "a planned event."

> The power outage <u>occurred</u> at approximately 3 p.m.
>
> Opening ceremonies will <u>take place</u> tomorrow afternoon at 2.

off of   Be wary of prepositions that enjoy one another's company. You may be practicing grammatical "featherbedding"—having two do the job of one. *Off of* is one of those redundant, bulky constructions. *Off* suffices.

> Get off (of) my back!
>
> Driscoll walked off (of) the stage and never performed again.

We are also suspicious of the phrase *across from*. However, the insertion of an object between these two words solves the awkwardness of the construction.

> The appliance store is across from the pharmacy.
>
> The appliance store is across <u>the street</u> from the pharmacy.

The addition of two words does not hurt the conciseness of the sentence. It certainly helps its clarity.

one of the/the only one of the Making a verb agree in number with its subject is not difficult—once you identify the proper subject. When the subject is a pronoun (*who* or *that*, for example) that refers to a noun elsewhere in the sentence, the task is somewhat challenging. Subject-verb agreement then depends on determining the correct antecedent. For *one of the/only one of the*, follow these rules:

1. In *one of the* constructions, the relative pronoun refers to the *object* of the preposition of the main clause, not the *subject*.

> Brock is <u>one</u> of the best <u>ballplayers</u> who have
> (subj.)   (obj. of prep.) (pron.) (verb)
> played the game in the last 50 years.

> (If you examine this sentence, you will see that Brock is not the only ballplayer who has played the game in 50 years. We are talking about *many players* who *have* played the game in that period. We are saying that Brock is included in that group.)

2. In *the only one of the* constructions, the relative pronoun refers to the *subject* of the main clause.

> <u>Jennings</u> is <u>the only one</u> of the candidates who   has
>   (subj.)   (pron.) (verb)
> opposed the nuclear freeze referendum.

> (There were no other candidates who opposed this referendum. The antecedent clearly is *Jennings*.)

For more information, see p. 65.

parallel structure When you place like ideas in like grammatical patterns, you create parallel structure. This consistency among elements gives order to your writing and helps make the message clear. Parallelism also creates balance, symmetry—and sometimes rhythm—in a sentence. Common errors in parallelism include mixing elements in a series, mixing verbals and switching voice.

For more information, see pp. 67 and 155.

parentheses Journalists use parentheses sparingly in their writing because the reason for their use—to provide additional information or an aside for the sentence—is generally contrary to brief, crisp writing. For those rare occasions when you do use them, here is a simple rule concerning punctuation: Put the period inside the parentheses only if the parenthetical material is a complete sentence and can stand independently of the preceding sentence.

> Don't fry onions in bacon grease. (You'll be asking for trouble.)

If these conditions are not met, the period goes outside.

> The funeralgoers chanted "Vaya con Dios" (Go with God).

See p. 122.

PE

people/persons   Some contend that a group is referred to as *people* but individuals are *persons.* We find it difficult to create a scale for acceptable use of *persons* (three? six?) and to set a cutoff point (seven people?), so it seems only reasonable to avoid the plural *persons.* Why do *seven persons* somehow have separate identities, but *28 people* do not? After many years of using *persons,* the Associated Press Stylebook now agrees with us. Save yourself the headache! There are more pressing decisions in life. If you are referring to "an individual," you are referring to a *person.*

> MacNelly thought the president was a kind person but an inept leader.

If you are referring to "more than one," you are referring to *people.*

> Four thousand people demonstrated at the Capitol today in opposition to welfare cuts.

per   This Latin preposition, meaning "through, by, by means of," is used today only when scientific or technical writing calls for it or when the Latin phrase associated with it fits the context of the story. Whereas we still use terms such as *miles per gallon, per capita* expenditures and *percent,* we do not say *$40 per day* or *$18,000 per year.* If you can replace *per* with the indefinite article *a* or *an* without awkwardness, do it.

possessives Chapter 5 discusses in detail the formation of possessives. One point about them, however, deserves emphasis: Possessives of personal pronouns are not the same as contractions.

Remember that the personal pronoun possessives (*my, mine, our, ours, your, yours, his, her, hers, its, their, theirs*) do not require an apostrophe. See p. 83 and the entry for *its/it's*.

preventive/preventative Why in the world use *preventative?* It uses two extra letters and still means *preventive!* It's pretentious, that's why. Practice preventive language arts—avoid overweight words.

principal/principle As a noun, *principal* means "someone who is first in rank or authority," such as the principal of a school. As an adjective, *principal* still means "first in rank or authority," such as the principal reason for the levy's defeat. *Principle,* however, is only a noun. It means "a truth, doctrine or rule of conduct," such as "an uncompromising principle of honesty." Obviously, the only thing common to these two words is their sound.

prior to Use *before*. *Prior to* is stuffy and falsely formal.

proved/proven Current use supports *proved* as the past participle of the verb *prove*.

Chrysler <u>has proved</u> the merits of its ad campaign.

Proven, although cited by some dictionaries as an acceptable alternate for the past participle, is preferred in journalistic style as an adjective only.

The Nike running shoe is a <u>proven</u> success.

In a linking verb construction then, you use *proven* if it takes the role of the predicate adjective:

Nike's success is <u>proven</u>.

(In this sentence, *proven* is not part of the verb. It is an adjective that modifies *success.*)

quotation marks   One of the most common concerns about quotation marks is where to place other marks of punctuation. Here is a brief recap:

1. Periods and commas always go inside.

2. Question marks and exclamation marks go inside if they are part of the quoted material.

The most common error in quotation mark punctuation is in placement of the question mark. Two examples show the correct placement:

> The senator asked the nervous lobbyist: "Can you honestly tell me that your baby food formula has never caused the death of a child in a Third World country?"

(The question mark belongs inside because it is part of a quoted question.)

> Have you seen all the toys modeled after "Rambo"?

(The entire sentence is a question; the title is declarative.)

See Chapter 7 for more information on quotation marks and other marks of punctuation.

quotation/quote   *Quotation* is a noun. *Quote* is a verb. However, the twain meet in newsrooms, where *quote* is often used as a noun. ("Get me some good quotes for this piece. It's dying of boredom.") Journalists are economical souls. That's why the verb *quote* has been changed to suit the purposes of the secret language of the newsroom. We urge you to keep the use there. In any writing for the non-initiated public, remember to quote only the good quotations.

ravage/ravish   To *ravage* is to destroy or ruin.

> A string of tornadoes <u>ravaged</u> the small Illinois town of Conant.

To *ravish* is to carry away forcibly or to rape.

> The conquering army <u>ravished</u> the Trojan women.

rebut/refute   It's easier to rebut a statement than to refute it. When you *rebut* a statement, you contradict it or deny it. But that doesn't mean you have done so successfully. When you *refute* a statement, you conclusively prove that you are correct. Use *refute* in your newswriting only if there is a consensus that the denial has been successful. Don't make the judgment on your own.

reluctant/reticent   People who are reluctant to do something are not necessarily reticent. A *reluctant* person is unwilling to do something.

> At first, Hart was <u>reluctant</u> to enter the presidential race.

If a person is unwilling to speak readily or is uncommonly reserved, we generally describe that person as *reticent*.

> The professor has instituted a class for <u>reticent</u> speakers.

renown/renowned   Often confused, these two words are different parts of speech. *Renown,* the noun, means "fame or eminence." *Renowned,* the adjective, means "famous or celebrated."

> <u>Renowned</u> scientist Linus Pauling won <u>renown</u> for his ground-breaking work in chemistry.

restrictive/non-restrictive   These high-sounding terms refer to the role of phrases and clauses in a sentence. A *restrictive clause* is an essential clause that helps define the meaning of a sentence. Identifying this type of clause helps you in two ways:

1. The restrictive clause does not need to be set off by commas.
2. In a choice between *that* and *which, that* is always the correct pronoun subject or object.

> The poll <u>that the senator commissioned</u> has not gone well for her.
>
> (The restrictive clause is underlined; without it, the sentence lacks definition.)

A *non-restrictive clause* is not essential to the context of the sentence. It must be set off by commas, and you use *which* instead of *that* when the choice has to be made.

Political polls, which are a staple of modern campaigning, are an important key to party fund raising.

(The non-restrictive clause is underlined; the sentence can be understood without it.)

run-on sentence   Like the boorish practical joker, it doesn't know when to stop. The run-on may actually be several sentences rolled into one and molded into an amalgam of confusion because of improper punctuation.

Picket lines went up for a fourth straight day, nurses vowed to continue to honor them until contract talks resume.

Use of a semicolon instead of a comma or insertion of the conjunction *and* after the comma would have corrected this fault. See also the entry for *comma splice* and pp. 43 and 110.

said   Don't overlook the use of this valuable verb when quoting someone. Searching for variety, writers sometimes reach out for *stated, uttered, elucidated, declared* or what have you. Describing the speaker and his or her delivery is more important than poring over a thesaurus to find a verb that is better off in a game of Scrabble than in journalistic writing. Also, don't overlook the value of quoting someone in the present tense. See p. 67 for a discussion of *says*.

semicolon   This important tool will help you avoid the run-on sentence. When two independent clauses are in one sentence and are not separated by a conjunction such as *and, but,* or *or,* they must be separated by a semicolon:

He is not your ordinary movie star; he is already a legendary figure in cinema.

When two independent clauses are joined by a conjunctive adverb such as *however, nevertheless* or *therefore,* a semicolon also is needed:

I can't speak for this faculty; however, I am adamantly opposed to any reduction in our humanities program.

set/sit   Normally, the verb *set* requires an object:

> Please <u>set</u> the <u>package</u> on the table.

Sit, however, never takes an object:

> Won't you please <u>sit</u> down?

since/because   These words are not synonymous. *Since* is best used when it denotes a period of time, whether continuous or broken.

> It has been many years <u>since</u> we have had a balanced budget.

Because gives a reason or cause.

> We haven't had a balanced budget <u>because</u> the government can't control its spending.

Note that in most circumstances, a comma is not needed before *because*.

so   This is a weak conjunction when it means "with the result that." It isn't strong enough to coordinate two independent clauses in one sentence.

> Lasorda couldn't decide whether Cey or Lopes should bat fourth, <u>so</u> he flipped a coin to speed his decision.

You will find that a rewrite is more direct and economical:

> Lasorda flipped a coin to see whether Cey or Lopes would bat fourth.

Another choice—and more direct than the *so* solution—is:

> <u>Because</u> Lasorda couldn't decide whether Cey or Lopes should bat fourth, he flipped a coin.

split constructions   The *split infinitive* is a usual topic in grammar texts. However, the chief reason for objecting to the split infinitive—loss of clarity—is also the reason for avoiding unnecessary splits of *a subject and verb* and of *a verb and its complement.* When writing these constructions, be aware of a loss of clarity when the split becomes awkward. Some examples:

The Cubs pledged <u>to</u> before the end of the month <u>break</u> their losing streak.

(A split infinitive—insertion of two prepositional phrases between the two parts of the verb—causes confusion.)

<u>Benson</u>, before switching to the Minolta line of equipment and commercially endorsing it, <u>used</u> "plate cameras" early in his career.

(A *split between subject and verb*—although not unusual—is awkward when it causes the reader to lose track of the thought.)

Prime Minister Thatcher reportedly <u>objected</u>, in a secret meeting with French diplomats held yesterday morning, to recent European <u>trade agreements</u>.

(A *split between the verb and its complement* disturbs the natural flow by injecting lengthy explanatory material.)

Clarity and flow are the key issues. Obviously, strict adherence to a "no splits" policy can lead to unimaginative writing. See p. 152.

than/then *Than* is used as a conjunction of comparison, although some grammarians say it can be a preposition if the clause of comparison is understood. Rather than deal with all of that here, our point is that *then*—an adverb denoting time—is often confused with *than.* If you are comparing something, use *than:*

No one is more aware of America's breakfast-eating habits <u>than</u> the fast-food magnates.

Then, on the other hand, carries the sense of "soon afterward":

First, we'll go to the art exhibit; *then* we'll try to get a table at that great Armenian restaurant.

(Note that *then* cannot connect these two independent clauses on its own. A semicolon is needed.)

When *than* is used to introduce an implied clause of comparison, the pronoun that may follow is most likely in the nominative case:

Tom is a lot smarter than <u>I</u> (am smart).

But some sentences won't permit this implied arrangement:

There is not a more dedicated student than <u>him</u>.

("Than he is a student" would not make sense here.)

For more information on this, see p. 79.

that/which/who   As the entry for *restrictive/non-restrictive* says, *that* is used to restrict meaning, and *which* is used to elaborate on it. These pronouns are used only in their particular types of clauses, but *who* can be used in both types when it refers to people or to things endowed by the writer with human qualities. Examples:

Construction bonds <u>that</u> are issued by local governments generally carry tax-free interest. (restrictive meaning)

Construction bonds, <u>which</u> can be a dependable tax shelter, carry different interest rates according to the credit standing of the local government. (nonrestrictive—gives explanation)

The people <u>who</u> interrupted the demonstration were arrested. (restrictive—in this case, *that* would be inappropriate)

Hollings, <u>who</u> is running for the State Senate seat from Culver City, charged this morning that the governor's office has been "grossly mismanaged." (non-restrictive—explanatory material follows *who*)

For a discussion of the selection of *who* and punctuation of these clauses, see pp. 77 and 105 and the entry for *restrictive/nonrestrictive*.

their/there/they're   Although they sound alike, these words have different functions in a sentence. *Their* is the possessive form of the pronoun *they*. It should cause little problem.

<u>Their</u> presentation is scheduled for 3 p.m.

(modifies the noun *presentation*)

When it begins a sentence, *there* is called an *expletive*. It is some-times called a *false subject* because it doesn't help determine the number of the verb.

There are only 26 shopping days until Christmas.

(Note that *days*, not *there*, controls the number of the verb.)

They're is a contraction of *they* and *are*, used only informally when you want to combine subject and verb:

"They're here," he said, looking out the window.

there are/there is   Beginning a sentence with the expletive *there* is generally an indirect and ineffective way to communicate. It adds clutter, not meaning. When you *have* to use it, however, be aware that *there* is not the subject of the sentence and does not control the number of the verb. In these sentences the subject usually follows the verb and controls its number.

There <u>are</u> many <u>ways</u> to fend off bankruptcy.
    (verb)   (subj.)

Generally speaking, only the first part of a compound subject following the verb in these sentences is used to determine the number of the verb.

There <u>is</u> too much <u>waste</u> and <u>inefficiency</u> in this company.
    (verb)   (subj.)   (subj.)

Remember the agreement rules of *there* constructions, but try to use these sentences sparingly. See p. 57.

toward/towards   Dictionaries call *towards* "archaic and rare." Save it for an antique convention.

try and/try to   Writing is more precise than speech. Although we may say—and hear—such sentences as "She will try and pass the test," this is neither good nor proper language use. When we write that someone is *attempting* something, we do not mean that

TH–
TR

the person is both trying *and* doing; we mean the person is trying *to* do something. It makes sense to introduce the infinitive with the preposition *to*.

> She will try <u>to</u> pass the test.

up   It can be anything but upbeat when it is coupled with a verb. Cluttered phrases such as *face up, slow up* and *head up* just slow down meaning.

> The administrator must <u>face up</u> to the inefficient operation of his department.

Why can't this administrator just *face* the inefficient operation? See p. 141.

very   Be very wary of intensifying adjectives with *very*. If you get used to the practice, you might very well be overlooking very much better, more precise adjectives and contributing to clutter. *Very* is only one example of an overused intensifier. Others are *really, completely, extremely* and *totally.* For example, rather than describing someone as *very sad,* you could choose these words: *depressed, melancholy, sorrowful* or *doleful.* See p. 143.

who's/whose   If you want the contraction, use *who's.*

> <u>Who's</u> speaking on the chicken dinner circuit tonight?
> (Who is speaking . . .)

If you need the possessive pronoun, use *whose.*

> <u>Whose</u> salmon boat has been reported missing?
> (To whom does that boat belong?)

If you want to use *whose,* it must modify something directly or by implication. In the preceding sentence, *whose* modifies *boat.*

who/whom   Although colloquial speech has done its best to eliminate *whom* from this handsome pair of pronouns, the case for their survival together remains strong. In most writing situations the use of *whom* does not seem elitist; it is merely correct.

<u>Whom</u> did the president name to his cabinet?

The use of *whom,* the objective case of *who,* shows the reader that the pronoun receives the action of the verb rather than initiates it. Similarly, avoiding the tendency to use the objective case improperly can show the reader that the action is beginning with the pronoun.

The jockey <u>who</u> the magazine said had thrown the race has been cleared by the state commission.

An analysis of this sentence reveals that *who had thrown the race* is a subordinate clause and that *the magazine said* is for attribution only and not part of the key structure of the clause. Obviously, proper selection of *who* and *whom* shows that you are a writer who understands the function of sentence parts. If you also want to utter such sentences as "Whom did you wish to see?" when someone comes to your door, well, that's up to you.

your/you're The same distinctions given in the entries for *their/they're* and *who's/whose* apply here. If you want to use the possessive form of the personal pronoun *you,* use *your.*

<u>Your</u> Freudian slips are showing. (modifies the noun *slips*)

If you want to compress (contract) the subject-verb *you are,* use *you're.*

<u>You're</u> going to be a great grammarian.

YO

APPENDIX

GRAMMAR, WORD-USE AND SPELLING EXAM

Relax! The following is a user-friendly test. You can take it as often as you want, and the answers are displayed as prominently as the questions. It is meant to be a diagnostic exam; we encourage you to take it *before* and *after* you study this book.

Page numbers are listed after each answer to refer you to a longer discussion of the item tested. If you choose an incorrect answer, review the cited material carefully until you understand the concept.

Good luck!

1. Ollie feels sick that John won the lottery. What part of speech is *sick?* (A) *noun;* (B) *adjective;* (C) *adverb.*

> ANSWER: (B) *adjective. Sick* modifies the proper noun *Ollie.* The relationship between *sick* and *Ollie* is connected by the linking verb *feels.* See p. 15.

2. Rebuilding her country's shattered economy is her chief goal. What part of speech is *Rebuilding?* (A) *noun;* (B) *verb;* (C) *adjective.*

> ANSWER: (A) *noun.* Remember that *-ing* words aren't always verbs. They can be adjectives (participles) if they modify a noun, or they can be nouns (gerunds)—as in this case, when *Rebuilding* is the subject of the sentence. See p. 18.

3. This is the kind of allegation that hounds a person for years. What part of speech is *that?* (A) *conjunction;* (B) *noun;* (C) *pronoun.*

> ANSWER: (C) *pronoun. That* is called a *relative pronoun* because it relates to an antecedent in another part of a sentence (in this case, the noun *allegation*). *That* is the subject of the sentence's subordinate clause and depends on its antecedent to determine the number of its verb. See pp. 21, 64.

4. Before he shot the president, Hinckley reportedly spent several days (A) *laying* (B) *lying* around his hotel room.

> ANSWER: (B) *lying.* This verb is intransitive, which means it doesn't have a direct object. *Lay* requires a direct object; *lie* does not. Whereas *lay* means "to place," *lie* means "to recline." See p. 15.

5. The stock market continued its phenomenal rally today (A), (B); trading exceeded 20 million shares.

> ANSWER: (B); This sentence has two independent clauses. They can be separated by a comma only if they are joined by a coordinating conjunction (*and, but, or, nor, for, yet,* or *so*). Without that conjunction, a semicolon is needed to create an abrupt break between these two complete thoughts. See pp. 45, 110.

6. *Acting on an anonymous phone call,* police today arrested prison escapee Harold Davis. The italicized sentence element is a (A) *verb;* (B) *subordinate clause;* (C) *participial phrase.*

> ANSWER: (C) *participial phrase.* The phrase acts as an adjective because it modifies the noun *police.* It is not a clause because it doesn't contain a subject and a verb. See p. 35.

7. He is a (A) *good natured* (B) *good-natured* (C) *good, natured* person.

> ANSWER: (B) *good-natured*. A compound modifier (in this case, an adjective modified by an adverb—both of which modify the noun *person*) is hyphenated unless part of that modifier is an *-ly* adverb. See p. 119.

8. (A) *Your* (B) *You're* going to be very sorry if you eat that pickled tofu.

> ANSWER: (B) *You're*. *Your* is a possessive pronoun, not a contraction of *you* and *are*. See p. 84.

9. Harmonicas, (A) *that* (B) *which* are simple to play, are great companions when you're stuck in Toledo.

> ANSWER: (B) *which*. The commas are your clue that some non-essential material has been set inside the main clause. The clause *which are simple to play* is not necessary to the meaning of the sentence; therefore, the relative pronoun *that* is not used. See p. 105.

10. The woman (A) *who* (B) *whom* detectives believed committed the robbery has been cleared.

> ANSWER: (A) *who*. You should separate and reconstruct the two clauses to analyze this answer. The independent clause is *The woman has been cleared*. The dependent clause, reconstructed, is *who committed the robbery, detectives believed*. The pronoun of choice, then, is *who* because it is the subject of *committed*. See p. 77.

11. She had a hard time accepting (A) *him* (B) *his* eating cold pizza for breakfast.

> ANSWER: (B) *his*. The personal pronoun *him* is in the objective case. However, the possessive pronoun *his* is needed here because it modifies the noun (gerund) *eating*. See p. 83.

12. None of his clothes (A) *is* (B) *are* likely to fetch more than 50 cents at a rummage sale.

> ANSWER: (B) *are*. This is one of those rare cases in which *none* takes a plural verb. In this sentence, you could not say "not one of his clothes *is*." Instead, *none* here means "not any of his clothes *are*." See p. 62.

13. Many people don't support the (A) *press'* (B) *press's* stance in the school board recall.

> ANSWER: (A) *press'*. Remember this rule: If a singular common noun ends in *s* and the next word begins with *s*, add only an apostrophe to form the possessive. See p. 85.

14. Rick always remembered this: (A) *The* (B) *the* fundamental things apply as time goes by.

ANSWER: (A) *The*. When a complete sentence follows a colon, its first letter is capitalized. See p. 113.

15. He called for his brother, for whom he had been searching all day (A), (B); but all he heard was the distant wail of a timber wolf.

ANSWER: (B); This is a compound-complex sentence (it has one dependent and two independent clauses). It also has internal punctuation before the needed semicolon. Such a sentence needs a more definite pause between thoughts, which a semicolon can provide. See p. 111.

16. (A) *"Its* (B) *"It's* just a matter of time until we can put together a winning season,"* the embattled athletic director told a quiet meeting of the alumni association.

ANSWER: (B) *It's*. The athletic director is saying *"It is* just a matter of time."* A contraction is needed, not the possessive *its*. See p. 84.

17. The criteria for judging the art contest (A) *was* (B) *were* never announced to the press.

ANSWER: (B) *were*. *Criteria* is the plural of *criterion*. Watch for unusual and foreign plurals when determining the number of the verb. See p. 61.

18. Three million board feet of California redwood (A) *was* (B) *were* exported last month.

ANSWER: (A) *was*. Although *feet* is a plural word, it has the meaning of a collective unit in this sentence. We get the sense of a large amount, not of many thousands of trees being shipped overseas. The intended meaning of a plural-sounding word may sometimes be singular. See p. 59.

19. The man (A) *who* (B) *whom* police arrested has confessed to the robbery.

ANSWER: (B) *whom*. *Whom* is receiving the action of the clause, *police arrested whom*. It must be in the objective case. The main clause is *The man has confessed to the robbery*. See p. 81.

20. Baseball is one of those games that (A) *don't require* (B) *doesn't require* extensive knowledge of its rules to enjoy it.

ANSWER: (A) *don't require*. The correct antecedent of the relative pronoun *that* is *games,* not *one*. There are several games that obviously don't require extensive knowledge of rules, if we understand the meaning of the sentence. The meaning would be different, of course, if the writer meant to say that baseball is *the only one* of the games that *requires* a good understanding of rules. See p. 65.

21. Neither the city councilors nor the mayor (A) *has* (B) *have* been linked to the concession contract scandal.

ANSWER: (A) *has*. When a compound subject (*councilors-mayor*) is in a *neither . . . nor/either . . . or* construction—or is separated by *but* or *or*—the part of the subject closest to the verb determines the number of the verb. See p. 61.

22. During the Great Depression, approximately two-thirds of the work force (A) *was* (B) *were* employed.

ANSWER: (A) *was*. When a word such as *half, plenty* or an actual fraction is the subject, the verb draws its number from the number of the prepositional phrase that follows the fraction. This, too, would be correct:

One-third of employable workers <u>were</u> without jobs during the Great Depression.

See p. 63.

23. Rains in the Midwest have delayed spring planting (A), (B); however, sunny skies are forecast for the rest of the week.

ANSWER: (B); When two independent clauses are not joined by a coordinating conjunction such as *and, but* or *or,* a semicolon is needed. The conjunctive adverb *however* is not strong enough to pull those two clauses together with a mere comma. See p. 111.

24. There is no better soccer player on the squad than (A) *she* (B) *her.*

ANSWER: (B) *her*. In this sentence, *than* is a preposition, not a conjunction of comparison. There is no implied comparison. You can't tack another clause ("than *she* is a soccer player") onto this sentence and have it make sense. See p. 79.

25. (A) *Whose* (B) *Who's* in charge here?

ANSWER: (B) *Who's*. The possessive *whose* doesn't modify anything in this sentence. The contraction of *Who is*—*Who's*—is needed here to provide subject and verb. See p. 84.

26. She is a (A) *widely-traveled* (B) *widely traveled* anthropologist.

ANSWER: (B) *widely traveled.* A compound modifier that has an *-ly* adverb in it does not require hyphenation. See p. 119.

27. Between you and (A) *me,* (B) *I,* the city's bond issue doesn't have a prayer at the polls.

ANSWER: (A) *me.* As the object of the preposition *between,* the pronoun must be in the objective case. See p. 81.

28. There (A) *was* (B) *were* some years when farmers lost money and had to borrow from the bank.

ANSWER: (B) *were. There,* an expletive, is not the subject of this sentence. In *there* constructions the true subject is usually preceded by the verb. In this sentence *years* is the subject and calls for a plural verb. See p. 57.

29. The agents are sworn to protect (A) *whoever* (B) *whomever* is elected to the office.

ANSWER: (A) *whoever.* This pronoun is the subject of the clause *whoever is elected to the office* and must be in the nominative case. See p. 79.

30. The president's speech was well-orchestrated, but not many senators were swayed by (A) *him* (B) *it.*

ANSWER: (B) *it.* The correct antecedent is *speech.* The possessive, *president's,* also modifies *speech.* See p. 64.

31. The news media (A) *is* (B) *are* not to blame for the current wave of doomsday attitudes.

ANSWER: (B) *are. Media* (the word) is the plural of *medium.* It normally takes a plural verb. See p. 61.

32. The number of bank failures (A) *has* (B) *have* increased this year.

ANSWER: (A) *has. The number* as a subject always takes a singular verb because its meaning is definite. *A number,* however, seems *less* specific and takes a plural verb. See p. 59.

33. Can you sit through "Gone with the (A) *Wind?"* (B) *Wind"?*

ANSWER: (B) *Wind"?* Question marks go inside quotation marks only if the quoted material is a question. Example:

The witness said, "Do you expect me to jeopardize the life of my brother?"

See p. 119.

34. None of her answers (A) *was* (B) *were* satisfactory.

ANSWER: (A) *was*. The indefinite pronoun *none* is a real trouble-maker because it takes either a singular or plural verb according to the meaning of the sentence. In this example, *none* means that "no one answer" was satisfactory. However, in "The master chef said that none of the pan juices were satisfactory," you can't read "no one pan juice." So the rule of "no amount" comes into play. If you can read "no amount" into a *none* construction, the verb should be plural. On occasion, a sentence may seem right with either the singular or plural verb; in that case, either stay with the singular or try to rewrite the sentence. See p. 62.

35. Focus the image, set the aperture and (A) *the shutter will trip when you press the button.* (B) *release the shutter by pressing the button.*

ANSWER: (B) *release the shutter*. . . . To maintain parallel structure in this sentence, keep the verb tense consistent. There is no reason to switch to the future tense here. The switch creates a break that disturbs the reader. Remember that consistency and clarity go hand in hand. See p. 67.

36. The (A) *warm northwest wind* (B) *warm, northwest wind* chased the Arctic chill that had gripped the area for two weeks.

ANSWER: (A) *warm northwest wind*. A comma is not needed between *warm* and *northwest* because they are not separate modifiers. You cannot call it a warm *and* northwest wind (substituting *and* is a technique for determining whether a comma is needed between modifiers). Actually, *warm* modifies the term *northwest wind*. A *warm, gentle breeze* is properly punctuated because *warm* and *gentle* separately modify *breeze*. See p. 106.

37. I can tell you are not (A) *averse* (B) *adverse* to constructive criticism.

ANSWER: (A) *averse*. It refers to a person's opposition or reluctance. *Adverse*, meaning "unfavorable or hostile," relates to things or concepts but never to people.

38. What (A) *affect* (B) *effect* do you think this will have on the team?

ANSWER: (B) *effect*. A *noun* is needed here to describe a result. *Affect* is almost always a *verb*.

39. I don't appreciate your attempts to (A) *allude* (B) *elude* to my criminal past.

ANSWER: (A) *allude*. An "indirect reference" is being made. *Elude* means "to escape."

40. Talks have resumed (A) *between* (B) *among* representatives of Argentina, Great Britain, the U.S. State Department and the United Nations.

ANSWER: (A) *between.* There is a *direct* relationship between the parties, even though there are more than two. *Among* is better used when the meaning "distribution" is intended.

41. A number of economic advisers (A) *has* (B) *have* abandoned the administration recently.

ANSWER: (B) *have. A number of* always takes a plural verb. If the article had been *the,* it would have taken a singular verb.

42. She is (A) *anxious* (B) *eager* to present her findings.

ANSWER: (B) *eager.* Because she is excited at the prospect of doing this, she is *eager.* If she were suffering from fear or anxiety, she would be *anxious.* You are eager *to do* something but anxious *about* something.

43. The aircraft spun dizzily toward the ground (A) *as if* (B) *like* it had been slapped by a giant hand.

ANSWER: (A) *as if.* It is a conjunction that introduces a clause, such as "it had been slapped." *Like* is used only as a preposition. It cannot introduce a clause.

44. Why did you select Susan for the committee rather than (A) *I* (B) *me?*

ANSWER: (B) *me.* If a comparison is being made, you use the nominative case ("Do you think Tom is as sensitive as I?"). But the meaning halts at the preposition *than* in this sentence. It requires a simple *object*—in the objective case. One test is to try to carry out the thought implied in the sentence. If you can expand the sentence, it probably requires the nominative case.

Do you think Tom is as sensitive as I? (am sensitive?)

Why did you select Susan for the committee rather than (I was selected?) (*Me* is needed here.)

45. Tom feels (A) *bad* (B) *badly* about his team's loss.

ANSWER: (A) *bad.* We are describing Tom's state in this linking verb construction. For example, we would not say "Tom feels sadly." An adjective, not an adverb, is called for.

46. His nightmares were (A) *because of* (B) *due to* his anxiety about his promotion.

ANSWER: (B) *due to.* You can't answer the question *why* in this construction. That's the main cue for using *due to.* In addition, the linking verb *were* needs an adjective to relate to nightmares. *Because of,* a preposition, doesn't fit the bill.

47. Dispatches from the fighting in the Mideast have been (A) *censored* (B) *censured* by government officials.

ANSWER: (A) *censored.* This information is being screened and edited, not condemned. People can be *censured* for their actions.

48. The speeding car (A) *collided with* (B) *crashed into* the telephone pole.

ANSWER: (B) *crashed into.* Both objects have to be moving in order to *collide.*

49. Fifty-six people died on the state's highways this Memorial Day, (A) *compared to* (B) *compared with* last year's count of 49.

ANSWER: (B) *compared with.* When you are making a side-by-side comparison to see similarities and differences, you use *compared with. Compared to* means "likened to."

50. The mayor's stubbornness can be (A) *compared to* (B) *compared with* the dead-set stance of a brick wall.

ANSWER: (A) *compared to.* In this sense, we are saying that the mayor's stubbornness can be "likened to" a brick wall. You can see that actual comparisons call for *compared with.*

51. Her success plan is (A) *composed of* (B) *comprised of* seven easy-to-learn steps.

ANSWER: (A) *composed of.* To begin with, *comprised of* is a redundant phrase. When *comprise* alone is used, it means "include." A more direct way to write this example is: "Her success plan *comprises* seven steps." When you want to say "is made up of," you choose *composed of.*

52. A (A) *continual* (B) *continuous* line of camels was silhouetted against the Saharan dusk.

ANSWER: (B) *continuous.* A continuous line is "unbroken." *Continual* means "repeated or intermittent":

Are your <u>continual</u> visits to the chiropractor really necessary?

Some stylists argue that the distinctions between *continuous* and *continual* are now blurred. We believe there are meanings here to be preserved—and Associated Press agrees.

53. I have been (A) *persuaded* (B) *convinced* that I must change my vote on this issue.

ANSWER: (A) *persuaded.* You receive persuasion; personal conviction is a state. You could say that you *are convinced* that a course of action is correct, but you could not *be convinced to* follow one.

54. Smith has always (A) *differed from* (B) *differed with* Taylor in temperament.

ANSWER: (A) *differed from.* Smith is not disagreeing with Taylor; these two people are merely unlike or dissimilar in temperament. Use *differ with* only to show argument or debate.

55. The (A) *enormity* (B) *enormousness* of the Mount Everest expedition has staggered even the most organized and experienced climbers.

ANSWER: (B) *enormousness.* We are talking about size—in this case, huge proportions. *Enormity* means "wickedness."

56. The forlorn-looking group moved (A) *further* (B) *farther* down the road.

ANSWER: (B) *farther.* We are discussing distance, not degree. There may seem to be distance associated with *further,* but it is more conceptual than concrete.

The planning subcommittee said it will study the recommendation **further.**

57. The candidate said this country needs (A) *fewer* (B) *less* welfare programs and more work-incentive projects.

ANSWER: (A) *fewer.* If you can get the sense of "specific or identifiable numbers," use *fewer.* Use *less* when you are talking about "amounts, quantity, sums and concepts." The following example shows this difference:

This country needs **fewer politicians** and **less politics.**

58. O'Shea reportedly (A) *hanged* (B) *hung* himself in his jail cell rather than face his embezzlement trial.

ANSWER: (A) *hanged.* People *hang* themselves. Whether it is by their own hand or by others', they are *hanged.* Pictures and other inanimate objects are *hung.* However, if O'Shea had been dead for several hours before his body was discovered, it would be correct to write that his body "*hung* in the cell for several hours."

59. Are you (A) *implying* (B) *inferring* that the treasurer's report is false?

> ANSWER: (A) *implying*. What is being questioned is "a hint or suggestion that apparently is being made." You can *infer* something ("make a deduction") from someone's implication. Think of *implying* as more direct and aggressive (as in "making a charge or accusation") and of *inferring* as more passive and contemplative ("figuring out what was meant by the implication").

60. The winning highway bid was (A) *less than* (B) *under* $45 million.

> ANSWER: (A) *less than*. Use *under* only if something is physically rather than figuratively under something else.
>
> **He was pinned <u>under</u> the wheels of the jackknifed trailer.**
>
> *Less than* always refers to "quantity or amount."

61. (A) *More than* (B) *Over* 5,000 demonstrators clogged downtown streets to protest the arrival of the nuclear submarine.

> ANSWER: (A) *More than*. Use the same logic as in the previous answer. Planes fly *over* mountains, but a budgeted figure is *more than* $2 million.

62. The four-car accident (A) *occurred* (B) *took place* on a foggy section of Interstate 405 near Tigard.

> ANSWER: (A) *occurred*. Use *take place* only to refer to something that has been scheduled.

63. Only 12 (A) *people* (B) *persons* attended the school budget meeting.

> ANSWER: (A) *people*. In the case of *person*, two's a crowd. If you have more than one person, you have *people*. It's a simple rule that will help you avoid unnecessarily complicated decisions.

64. His (A) *principals* (B) *principles* yielded like the skin of a rotten apple when he was offered fame and fortune.

> ANSWER: (B) *principles*. As the subject of the sentence, *principles* is a noun. *Principals* in this case would have meant "someone in authority," such as a school principal. But this sentence refers to "beliefs and rules of conduct"—*principles*, which can only be a noun. *Principal* can also be an adjective when it means "main or chief," as in "the *principal* reason for denying the petition."

65. In the opinion of courthouse regulars the prosecution has not (A) *proved* (B) *proven* that Robinson is an arsonist.

ANSWER: (A) *proved.* The preferred past and past perfect form of the verb *prove* is *proved.* However, *proven* can be used as an adjective, as in "something can be proven." (*Proven* modifies *something.*) As far as this sentence is concerned, if the prosecution has not *proved* guilt, then the defendant is not a *proven* arsonist.

66. (A) *Because* (B) *Since* the state is far behind in revenue collections, the governor will ask the legislature to convene.

ANSWER: (A) *Because. Since* should be used only to denote "a period of time."

The city has offered free parking <u>since</u> 1976.

Use *because* to indicate "a reason or cause."

67. The smell of gardenias invariably (A) *evokes* (B) *invokes* memories of the funeral.

ANSWER: (A) *evokes.* In this sentence, the gardenias are helping to "recall" memories of the funeral. To *invoke* would be to "call upon" or to "implore":

Athena <u>invoked</u> the power of the gods to help her retain her beauty.

68. She promised to (A) *lend* (B) *loan* me her car while mine was being repaired.

ANSWER: (A) *lend.* You can't go wrong using *lend* in all situations as a verb meaning "allow to borrow." However, *loan* is used as a verb in the context of a financial transaction:

The bank refused to <u>loan</u> him sufficient funds for the project.

Loan is generally a noun.

69. The goal of her Midwest whistle-stop tour was to (A) *elicit* (B) *illicit* $5 million in campaign funds.

ANSWER: (A) *elicit.* To *elicit* means "to draw forth" or "gather." *Illicit* is an adjective, not a verb. It means "improper or illegal."

70. An internationally (A) *renown* (B) *renowned* photojournalist, he is equally (A) *renown* (B) *renowned* for his arrogance.

ANSWER: (B) *renowned*—for both. *Renown* is a noun, as in "She is a writer of great *renown.*"

Note: Answers for the last 10 questions are at the end of this section. Look at each group of four words, and identify the misspelled word, if any. If you think a word is misspelled, spell it correctly. If you think that all words are correct, go to the next group.

71. desirable   excuseable   irresistible   noticeable

72. leisure   hygiene   yield   weird

73. relevant   persistant   resistant   superintendent

74. accumulate   separate   accomodate   appropriate

75. cancelled   omitted   traveled   committed

76. proceed   accede   precede   supersede

77. dilemma   broccoli   innoculate   vilify

78. protein   harrassment   recommend   questionnaire

79. batallion   medallion   sacrilegious   financier

80. judgement   commitment   occasion   ecstasy

ANSWERS:

71. excusable

72. all are correct

73. persistent

74. accommodate

75. canceled

76. all are correct

77. inoculate

78. harassment

79. battalion

80. judgment

Please count your correct answers for the entire test. If you received a score of 65 or better, you are showing some mastery of grammar, word use and spelling. However, remember that this is just one test; you will be tested *daily* in your writing and speech.

BE READY!

INDEX